RUNES

Thorsons
PRINCIPLES
OF

RUNES

FREYA ASWYNN

Thorsons

Thorsons
An Imprint of HarperCollins*Publishers*
77–85 Fulham Palace Road
Hammersmith, London W6 8JB

The Thorsons website address is: www.thorsons.com

Published by Thorsons 2000
3 5 7 9 10 8 6 4 2

A catalogue record for this book
is available from the British Library

ISBN 0 7225 3883 9

Printed and bound in Great Britain by
Caledonian Book Manufacturing Ltd, Glasgow

CONTENTS

ACKNOWLEDGEMENTS

A special vote of thanks is hereby offered to Andrew Clifton for his inestimable help with proof-reading, to Offy Dvalinson who contributed to the aromatic correspondences, and to Kveldulfr Gundarsson for his marvellous contributions to this work.

Also a vote of thanks to Llewellyn publishers for their cooperation.

ABOUT THE AUTHOR

F reya Aswynn was born in Holland in November 1949 to a
strict Roman Catholic family. As a child she displayed
natural psychic abilities, and this, combined with her reac-
tions to a hostile family environment, prompted the official
diagnosis that she was 'maladjusted'. Entrusted to the so-called
'care' system, she was institutionalized for nine years. Her intelligence, combined with a capacity for aggressive self-assertion,
allowed her to emerge from this ordeal more or less psychologically unscathed at the age of 19. Deprived of any secondary
education, she resorted to taking on cleaning work, until she
met and married her first husband, George. Somewhat older in
years, George introduced her to the basics of philosophy (particularly the works of Friedrich Nietzsche) and classical music,
predominantly Richard Wagner. He was also the first person to
speak to her about the esoteric nature of the runes. Sadly, after
two years of marriage, George died of cancer; but he left Freya
with a pension that, for the first time, gave her a measure of
financial independence.

Determined now to make good her lack of learning, Freya
taught herself English and German by means of books and
tapes. At the same time, she took an interest in the development
of her long-suppressed psychic gifts. She received her first

paranormal training in a spiritualist environment, and from there progressed to the study of Rosicrucianism, astrology and Cabbala. At the age of 30, she felt unable to progress further in Holland and left for England, where she was soon was recognized by prominent magicians and witches as a natural. With their help and training, she was initiated into the mysteries and made rapid progress as a ritual magician.

The next major turning-point for Freya was a life-changing spiritual and magical experience: an intense, spontaneous invocation of the God Woden. She took this to be a calling to open up the Northern pathway which, until then, was virtually non-existent within the occult community. She embarked on an intensive study of the runes and began work on her first book, *Leaves of Yggdrasil* (revised and updated in 1998 under the title *Northern Mysteries and Magick*). Within Pagan circles, this initiative was at first viewed with scepticism and suspicion as to whether she had a covert political agenda (which at that time was often the case with Odinists). Freya soon overcame these perceptions and won the respect and affection of the majority of the Pagan and occult community.

On a social level, realizing that she was not suited to living in a normal nuclear family, Freya became actively involved with a community which she ran for a number of years as Managing Director, together with her partner Lionel Hornby and their friend Alison Behr, a professional librarian, well-known Jewish feminist activist and a supporter of gay and bisexual rights. During this period, Freya decided to choose a celibate path, for her own spiritual reasons. After Lionel's death in 1994, Freya sold her share in the property and in 1996 she bought a large farmhouse in Scotland and founded another community named 'Gladsheim'. Initially rather unsuccessful due to errors of judgement leading to financial losses, she soon pulled it around with the help of friends within the Scottish Pagan community, and as of now (1998/1999), Gladsheim is on the road to success once more.

In 1993, Freya had started up a UK branch of the Ring of Troth, originally an American organization founded by Edred Thorsson and James Chisholm. The UK branch soon attracted members in other European countries and, re-named the Ring of Troth Europe, rapidly became a successful and progressive Northern Tradition group. Having led this organization as Steerswoman for a number of years, Freya stepped down from this role and other positions of power. She now concentrates on teaching and guiding as an Elder in the Ring of Troth and is actively 'on call' to members for advice and counsel when required.

Strathaven 1999.

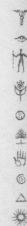

ORIGINS OF THE RUNES

HISTORICAL ORIGINS OF THE RUNES

In Middle-Earth (Middle Earth and Midgard are terms synony-
mous with 'earth'), the runes probably became known to
humans some time between the first century BCE and the end of
the first century CE. Some rune signs are, however, much older
than that and have been found all over the world, from Indo-
European settlements to Newgrange in Ireland. Their shapes —
vertical staves with slanted cross-cuts — show that they were
designed to be cut into wood, but because of difficulties in
preservation, the oldest inscriptions that have survived are in
metal and stone (with the exception of some Frisian staves
which were preserved by peat bogs). Some elements of runic
writing are almost certainly derived from Mediterranean alpha-
bets (Roman, Greek, and North Italic have all been discussed as
hypothetical models); others, from the Bronze Age stone-signs
of the Germanic peoples. Their use and understanding, however, are thoroughly Germanic; and as tools of magic, suitable for
memorial and operative inscriptions, they were naturally
known as the gift of the god Wodhanaz to his people. According
to the Norse poem 'Hávamál' Odhinn won the runes through a
shamanic initiation of fasting and death upon the world-tree,

through which he reached down to the deepest roots of the origins of the cosmos to draw up their holy pattern. The pattern of Wyrd.

'Wyrd' is the unseen web of synchronicities, originating in the Well of Wyrd. Each person, as well as collectives, adds layers to the Well of Wyrd through actions and this will manifest as a result. There is a similarity with 'karma', although wyrd is completely impersonal and non-judgemental in the dualistic sense.

The oldest runes known to us are those of the Elder Futhark ('futhark' is the runic equivalent to 'alphabet', derived from the first six runes — F, U, Th, A, R, and K/C), a 24-rune pattern divided into three aetts ('eights' or 'families'). This futhark was most likely developed in the second century BCE for religious and magical purposes.

The so-called Younger Futhark developed in Scandinavia between the ninth and eleventh centuries, whereas the Anglo-Saxon futhark dates from approximately the seventh century and was well established by the tenth, having nine runes added to accomodate language changes and to simplify its use as an alphabet for mundane and legal writing. The Younger Futhark remained primarily in use for magic and was gradually reduced to sixteen runes. When it became too obscure to be used for writing, dots were added to distinguish some phonetic values.

The importance of the runic order and the division into aetts was so strong that even when the Scandinavian futhark (Younger Futhark) had been reduced to sixteen runes, not only the order but the division of the runes into three aetts survived, even though they no longer filled three 'eights'. The worst offence any modern practitioner has ever perpetrated against runic lore is to confuse the holy rune-row and change the ancient order of the futhark according to whim, destroying the pattern which held such great meaning to our forebears.

This has generated a huge burst of destructively chaotic energy in those unfortunate and gullible enough to accept this warped version without referring to any other works on the runes. It is the purpose of this book to bridge the gap between advanced books such as *Teutonic Magic* by Kveldulfr Gundarsson, *Futhark* and *Runelore* by Edred Thorsson and my own *Northern Mysteries*, and the mediocre rubbish which is so commonplace today. In this book I strive to make the runes accessible to those people who are sensitive to their energies and meanings without necessarily having to wade through the scholastic or deeply esoteric material available today, whilst maintaining the integrity of the runes and their applications.

As the original language of the North (Proto-Germanic or Common Germanic) developed in several different directions, the futhark also changed to reflect the shifting sounds of different dialects, though the basic order was always preserved. In north Germany, the Frisians and Anglo-Saxons added several runes to the futhark, a development which ultimately ended in the thirty-six rune Anglo-Saxon futhork (the old a-rune taking on the sound-value of o); in Scandinavia, as mentioned above, the system was simplified to sixteen runes. Like the futhark order and the division into aetts, the names of the individual runes were generally preserved, though the Anglo-Saxon futhork, written down in the Christian period, is thought to have substituted similar words for the rune-names Oss (As, 'god') and Tiw (Tyr, the god's name) to de-heathenize the original meanings. As the twentieth century draws to its close the runes enjoy a resurgence and are reaching a wider audience than at any time in the past thousand years. But that audience is different than that for which they were originally intended, and this has resulted in many different perspectives emerging and converging upon them, and consequently originated a whole new set of interpretations based on the Old Lore but re-evaluated and updated to modern usage.

There is nothing wrong with this as long as respect is paid to some of the basic principles which, although originating from our ancestral past, have stood the test of time, particularly the order of the futhark, the shapes of the runes and their names, albeit in different languages.

MYSTICAL ORIGINS OF THE RUNES

Runes have been around outside time and space since the origins of the universe itself. The signs used in the various futhark or futhorcs are the Germanic embodiment of these mysteries, as is borne out by the primary meanings of the word 'Rune' itself — secret, mystery and song. The runes are the song or sound of the 'becoming in existence' of the material universe in so far as we may know and understand this. The runes are the physical embodiment of the Mysteries of the origin of consciousness itself, in the form of Odin/Woden, the god mostly associated with the runes. Poetically, one could say that the runes are the DNA of Odin, within the context of Germanic understanding. It goes without saying that other tribal peoples have their own, often similar, systems of interpretation and understanding of these mysteries.

For the purpose of this book, whenever I say 'runes' I mean the pictographic sigils as they are known today.

Runes are a tool for communication, therefore they are a language, albeit a language of symbols rather than a language of letters. However, they also function in the latter manner as they can be used adequately to write with, as is known from the carvings and writings of the past. 'Rune' is often a descriptive term for an obscure, cryptic, unidentifiable sign referred to in science fiction, horror and fantasy literature. Most of the time these runes have nothing to do with the futhark runes, with the exception of course of Tolkien. These writers instinctively feel the hidden power of 'Runes', futhark or otherwise. Runes are a language of the most simple kind as much used for mundane and even profane sayings as they are a language of the deepest collective unconscious, submerged in mystery and fraught with hidden dangers. There is a dark Lovecraftian feel to 'Runes'. Some magicians may choose to work on these lines, I do not. I attempt to work with the runes for the advancement of understanding, personal spiritual growth, and communication with subtle realms of knowledge, power and might. Runes can be used equally to create a message to your kinsman asking him to 'feed the cat', and to create a message to your unconscious which will eventually manifest itself through the higher mind as, possibly, an insight or a teaching.

HISTORY OF THE RUNES, THEIR USE AND ABUSE FROM ANCIENT TO MODERN

We do not know much about the use of runes historically speaking, but some artefacts date from the second century EV (era vulgaris, commonly known as CE, common era, or AD, anno domini) with inscriptions including archaic names of Germanic gods. These may have been hallowed items of magic, which would indicate that they were used in a religious and/or magical context. From at least the second century onwards they were a hidden tradition, not accessible to everyone. Most magical traditions, by the time they emerge in the outer world, have already had a hidden existence for some time. We will never know this for sure, but could all the runes have appeared almost overnight in a neatly outlined row of 24! Just like that? It is not very likely.

We know from the Roman Tacitus, who lived around 98 CE, that runes or 'notea' were used for divination in a specific manner. When the Roman Christians enslaved and subverted

6 our nations the runes went underground and, much later in the Middle ages, re-emerged as Masonic marks. In Iceland in the dark ages the possession of runes actually carried a death penalty similar to the death penalty for 'witchcraft' in the rest of Europe. We still have similar laws by which possession of certain herbs and plants still carries penalties. Evolution of consciousness and freedom takes a long time indeed. Perhaps 500 years from now we too will be viewed as a 'dark age'!

So, the runes were 'used' for magic, religion, divination and writing. The runes were also abused by the Nazis, who misappropriated them and attempted to pervert their meaning to fit in with their despicable political objectives, and inevitably paid the price for their foolishness, proving that the runes are not to be messed with. We Asatruar are followers of the Northern god/desses — the term 'Asatru' literally translates as 'True to the gods (aesir)'. We are, for the most part, born after the war and only familiar with its events via second-hand education and information, and are often lumped in with the Nazi spectre. This brings our integrity into question far more than those practising other forms of Paganism.

SETTING THE RECORD STRAIGHT!

The runes are the holiest, mightiest and highest emanations of the consciousness of the Gods, whatever one perceives these to be. They are there for those who feel inclined towards them as a mystery path of empowerment and evolution. No one human being may say 'No' to any other, using the runes! Misuse of the runes, as I have said, will carry its own retribution. Race or sex bear absolutely no relevance to the use of runes! Culture may play a part, but certain cultures may interface and correspond with each other. Cultures based in masculine monotheism are generally the exception to this.

4PRINCIPLES OF RUNES

TRADITIONAL MEANINGS OF THE RUNES

I n this chapter I will look at the most basic and literal meanings of the runes, with the minimum of interpretation. Later, I will explore some of the deeper meanings of the runes, when I discuss how to work with them in divination and magic.

The oldest version of the runes is known as the Common Germanic (or Elder) Futhark. The word 'Futhark' derives from the names of the first six rune names. The 24 runes of the Elder Futhark are divided into three groups of eight known as Aetts. 'Aett' translates roughly as 'family' and this indicates that the eight runes in each aett form a group and have something in common.

FIRST AETT

Germanic name: FEHU
Anglo-Saxon name: FEOH
Old Norse name: FE
Phonetic value: F
Traditional meaning: Cattle; wealth

The first aett is named after the Vanic God Frey: 'Frey's aett'. Personally I have always felt that this includes his twin sister Freyja. The classical meaning of Fehu as handed down through various sources is cattle or wealth, in particular, movable wealth, and therefore by implication, perishable wealth. In a so-called primitive society such as existed in Northern Europe at the time when the runes were first developed, cattle represented wealth. The status of the chieftain was usually measured by the number of cattle which he or she owned. In those days, cattle provided both a livelihood and a barter medium used in much the same way as money is used nowadays. The present-day English word 'fee' is a reminder of the name of this rune.

Today, the meaning of money itself has undergone many mutations. From coins made of metal and notes made of paper we are now moving into the era of digital money: plastic 'smart-cards' and meaningless figures stored somewhere in cyber-space. Only time will tell whether this is an improvement. This brings to mind an overlooked but pertinent aspect of the Fehu rune, namely, its relevance to the food chain. Cattle eat grain, as do we; and in spite of fears about BSE, most of us still eat beef — or at least milk, cheese and other dairy products derived from cattle. So, food is energy recycling in many forms, and in fact, food is the real bottom line with the Fehu rune. Money is ultimately useless in itself: you can't eat paper or metal, let alone figures on some computer! I urge everyone who works with Fehu to emphasize food rather than money, for physical as well as spiritual well-being. Synchronistically, the shape of the Fehu rune resembles an ear of wheat.

Fehu is the rune which embodies 'Hamingja', which is the source of personal power and 'luck' inherent in each person. We each inherit a store of Hamingja at birth from ancestors and from previous lives, and this may be added to by acts of might and honour or diminished by acts of weakness and dishonour.

Germanic name: URUZ
Anglo-Saxon name: UR
Old Norse name: UR
Phonetic value: U
Traditional meaning: Aurochs

The Aurochs was a ferocious native species of wild ox similar to a European bison which is now extinct. In olden days, in Continental Germania, the young warriors were subjected to a test of strength, an ordeal in which they had to go out armed with only the most basic weapons and single-handedly slay one of these beasties, bringing back the horns as proof that they had succeeded. (The horns were highly prized as drinking vessels.) The hunting and slaying of the Aurochs with a spear or knife was a risky business, and probably the chances of success were not very great. Having succeeded, the boy had presumably endured a rite of passage and was accepted into the tribe as a adult warrior.

The task of hunting, tracking and slaying an Aurochs demanded strength, endurance, patience and above all courage. These are the values embodied and encoded in the rune. Uruz is a direct representation of the life force pertaining to physical health.

Character values belonging to this rune are stamina, independence, endurance, the ability to take responsibility and the ability to control aggression.

Perhaps there is a shamanic connection with this rune such as exists in Native American buffalo lore. Before the religion of the Aesir in Germany, back in Neolithic times when the Aurochs was still roaming free, this animal may have been seen as a manifestation of the horned god of nature or the Wild Man of the Woods; a very early form, perhaps, of Wodan.

Germanic name: THURISAZ ᚦ
Anglo-Saxon name: THORN
Old Norse name: THURS
Phonetic value: TH
Traditional meaning: Giant

Thurisaz is the oldest Germanic word for 'Giant' — also known as a 'Jotun' in Old Norse or 'Eoten' (Middle-English 'Ettin') in Anglo-Saxon. In *Leaves of Yggdrasil* I speculated that the rune represents a 'Giant' god or god of the Giants; thus Thurisaz is mostly connected with Thor. Whilst writing this it occurs to me that it equally well may have connection with Loki in his Utgard Loki aspect, where he appears as a giant. Certainly the aggressive form of the fire element, mostly in destructive form, would support this possible interpretation.

Giants are representative of the forces of chaos as opposed to order in Norse cosmology. They are, however, not to be viewed as 'the enemy' in a strict black/white dualistic system, but rather should be viewed as necessary participating forces of evolution: chaos and order, gods and giants form an interwoven pattern in perpetual flux, as seen in nature itself. Thurisaz is the most destructive rune, representing natural forces, from erupting volcanoes to hurricanes and floods; these all may be symbolized by giants on the rampage. However, it seems to me that in this day and age, these giant forces are not necessarily opposing the gods, but rather they might be attempting damage control to offset the incredible destruction wrought by ... yes, humans! Perhaps the gods and the giants have formed an uneasy alliance to save as much of the planet as possible!

Germanic name: ANSUZ ᚨ
Anglo-Saxon name: OS
Old Norse name: ASS
Phonetic value: A
Traditional meaning: Ancestor/god

The fourth rune of the futhark is complimentary in its meaning to the previous one, representing order and the gods, especially Odin. The Ansuz rune represents consciousness, intelligence, communication and reason.

The element of Odin, the god-force behind this rune, is Air. Air is a penetrating medium necessary to all life-forms. It is through air that sound becomes audible. In an airless environment, sound cannot be heard, and sound is the other main feature of the Ansuz rune, including the origins of sound as a medium of communication between people, and the sounds of Nature. The magical use of sound to expand one's consciousness and the chanting of runes in a manner in which sound is closely linked with breath can give spectacular results.

Ansuz is derived from the proto-Germanic word 'Ansus' which means 'ancestor' and in the Northern Mysteries the God most frequently seen as a divine ancestor is Odin. Our gods may have originated as ancestral spirits which gradually acquired divine attributes. The gods themselves have changed and evolved as human understanding of them has changed and developed over the centuries. Even in one lifetime, such change takes place, and after all my experiences of working with Odin, I find myself continually redefining him in my own understanding. Beyond mine or anybody else's understanding of him is the greater mystery of his being which cannot be fully comprehended by incarnate spirits such as humans.

The Anglo-Saxon traditions calls this rune 'mouth' ie the origin of speech. Speech is one of Odin's attributes, as are

poetry and the aforementioned magical uses of sound. It is no coincidence that Odin, the god of words and communication, is credited with giving mankind knowledge of the runes. The extra dimension of knowledge gained when discussing the runes with a like-minded individual illustrates the communicative aspect of Odin as the power of consciousness.

> Germanic name: RAIDO ᚱ
> Anglo-Saxon name: RAD
> Old Norse name: REID
> Phonetic value: R
> Traditional meaning: Riding

The traditional and accepted meaning of this, the fifth in the futhark, is 'Ride', originally referring to long journeys on horseback or in a chariot such as some of our gods and goddesses were known to use. Odin, for example, travels on Sleipnir, his eight-legged horse; Thor travels in a chariot drawn by goats and Freyja likewise travels in a chariot drawn by cats. Raido thus represents both means of transport and the activity of journeying. Mythically, it is also associated with 'Asgard's Ride' in Scandinavia, which was known in German and British folklore as the 'Wild Hunt': the wintry ride of Odin and his retinue of battle-slain warriors, manifested in the winds and storms of Yule-tide.

Riding has also connotations of creating movement, generating motion, taking charge of situations, being in control, taking the initiative, starting a new venture, decision-making or directing a course of action.

Rad, the Anglo-Saxon name of the rune, is cognate with the German Rat and Dutch raad, meaning 'counsel' or 'advice', which is one of the other meanings of Raido. It gives sound advice in a reading. There happens to be another word of

Gothic origin, 'raiht', which in my opinion is closely related to rad or Raido. This word means 'right', or in Dutch 'recht', the related verb being rechten, meaning in English 'to do right, to dispense judgment, to litigate'. The Dutch word for 'judge' is rechter.

Raiht is linked to the institution of kingship. In the old days, kings had the task of dispensing justice. The Latin word for king, 'rex', derives from the same root source as raiht, as does Heimdallr's alternative name 'Rig' in the Eddic poem 'Rigisthula', in which this enigmatic god is seen as the originator of the three main divisions of society: thralls, farmers and rulers.

All these associations explain why Raido is a rune that speaks to us of leadership and nobility. In olden times, nobility was not something which was automatically acquired by virtue of birth. Rather, it was a position which was earned or held by merit, and it implied moral responsibility and integrity. Raido refers to the correct balance between respecting the rights of others and respecting one's own individual rights.

Germanic name: KENAZ 〈
Anglo-Saxon name: CEN
Old Norse name: KAUN
Phonetic value: K or hard C
Traditional meaning: torch, light

Most rune-workers interpret the meaning of the Kenaz rune as 'torch', which has always been regarded as a symbol of knowledge, consciousness and intellect. Kenaz means 'to know'; the Scottish dialect verb 'ken' and the Dutch and German 'kennen' all mean 'to know, to be familiar with', but also connote skills and abilities, ie 'to be able to'. The English word 'cunning' is etymologically derived from the same root as Kenaz.

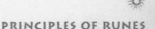

Kenaz therefore implies the acquisition and application of knowledge. The terms 'cunning man' or 'cunning woman' were often used as euphemisms for 'witch', denoting someone skilled in magic, herb-craft, or other 'specialist' knowledge more or less occult, especially when it concerned the hidden knowledge of a female nature. There is a certain English word, often used as a crude expletive and derived from the same Indo-European root-word as Kenaz, which demonstrates both the femininity of this kind of intuitive knowledge and also the extent to which it has been denigrated and de-valued in our culture.

While Raido is the rune which directs us towards the right path, Kenaz sheds light on this path so that we may know where we are going. Together, they can guide us in the proper direction.

The rune's element is fire in its contained form, that is to say the fire of enthusiasm and inspiration. One of the gods who can be successfully invoked with a Kenaz working is HeimdallR, who is known as the 'Shining God'. He is the god who, in the Eddic poem 'Rigisthula', teaches the runic mysteries to the child Kon — whose name is etymologically related to Kenaz, and whose descendants become kings and rulers.

Thus, Kenaz is associated with the transmission of knowledge — the passing on of the torch to the next generation of kin or cyn. Both of these words are of Anglo-Saxon origin and are related to Kenaz. As such it indicates the learning and teaching process. The Old English word cyning is also related to Kenaz. Cyning meant king. The king, according to tradition, had to be a descendant of Woden. He acted as the focal point of the collective folk-soul, for the king was the torch-bearer of the folk's consciousness and conscience.

Germanic name: GEBO X
Anglo-Saxon name: GIFU
Old Norse name: none
Phonetic value: G
Traditional meaning: Gift

This rune, the seventh of the futhark, is named Gifu in Anglo-Saxon, and means a gift, or giving. All energy systems are exchange mechanisms; we take, we give, we trade. The life force itself ebbs and flows in us in this way as we interact with our environment, even at the most basic level of breathing in oxygen and breathing out carbon dioxide. Plants complement our interaction with the atmosphere by assimilating carbon dioxide and exchanging this for oxygen; thus a balance is maintained. Similar processes of exchange are constantly active in us, sustaining life and consciousness. When we enter this life, we are endowed with 'gifts': talents, abilities, etc.

These gifts are passed on from our particular ancestors, and in general from the collective genetic pool whose origins lay with the gods themselves. Metaphorically, we are certainly descended from our gods. Perhaps this is true genetically as well; it all depends on one's point of view and whether one can envisage the possibility of the gods at some point in history having had a physical existence. At any rate, we are endowed with gifts, from the start, and these gifts have to be passed on in one form or another.

Having received such gifts, we are obliged to give in our turn, both to the gods in the form of sacrifice, which can mean anything from a flower or a glass of drink before a statue to a commitment to a project and seeing it through. The Gebo rune teaches us to become conscious of the process of exchange in all its forms. It teaches us not to take more than we are willing

to give, for when we create an imbalance, we shall have to compensate for that at some time or another.

Sometimes the compensation required can take a different form and be extracted on a different level. If we eat more than our bodies need, sooner or later — sometimes much later — our bodies will object to the abuse and give us trouble in the form of illness. This is a simple example of the natural working of the Gebo rune.

The shape of the rune is perfect balance in all four directions, it is symmetrical and bilateral, above, below, left and right all look exactly the same. The rune is neutral, it is neither a 'good' rune nor a 'bad' one, simply indicating equilibrium and balance. Giving and receiving in equal measure.

Giving does not exist in a vacuum, even if it does not look for overt payment or recompense, because the giver needs to receive something back — even if this is only an emotional benefit. In this realistic view, altruism in the sense of absolute self-lessness cannot exist and would be out of balance. Everything in nature, everything in the soul and everything in mind seeks its equal and opposite for complimentary equilibrium.

Germanic name: WUNJO ᛈ
Anglo-Saxon name: WYNN
Old Norse name: none
Phonetic value: W and sometimes V
Traditional meaning: Joy

The name of this rune is usually translated by other rune-workers as 'joy' or 'pasture'. This association with joy is evidently derived from the rune-name's similarity to the modern German word 'Wonne', which may indeed be derived from the proto-Germanic word Wunjo. Although this interpretation is not altogether wrong, the original meaning of the word Wunjo in the oldest Germanic language known to us is 'perfection', according to the philologist Jacob Grimm. A variant of this word is 'Wunsch' which means wish. From the combination of these words one can deduct that Joy is attained when fulfilment of Wish has occurred and thus both meanings, ancient and modern, converge neatly.

The key to joy then is the ability to wish, the correct application of the will or 'intent'. The reason most people are unhappy is that they are discontent and wish for the impossible, and then rage in frustration at wyrd when they are disappointed. I think the lesson in Wunjo is to wish wisely, and be content with what little joys and comfort wyrd may bestow on you. The Anglo-Saxon name for the rune, 'wynn', may originally have been 'wenn', which supports the above as 'wenn' also means 'hope' and expectation.

One of Odin's bynames is Oski, which means fulfiller of wishes. This corresponds to the German tradition expressed by the word 'Wunsch' which, like the English 'wish', and the Dutch 'wens', derives from the proto-Germanic word Wunjo, meaning 'perfection' or 'fulfilment'. Odin certainly has the power to grant 'wishes', but as the saying goes, be careful what you wish for — you might just get it!

What most people wish for more than any material wealth, beyond the everyday necessities of course, is companionship, in either a committed one-to-one relationship, or family bonding, or trusted friends and Kinfolk with shared ideals and objectives. Wunjo therefore also has been associated with fellowship and bonding of clan. Often groups affiliated for religious or spiritual reasons or even for something as common as football have a banner as a symbolic display of their shared identity and unison of will.

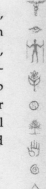

SECOND AETT

Germanic name: HAGALAZ ᚺ
Anglo-Saxon name: HAEGL
Old Norse name: HAGALL
Phonetic value: H
Traditional meaning: Hail

This is the first rune of the second aett: the aett of Hagalaz. This aett is named after an element, whereas the others are named after the gods Frey and Freyja for the first aett and Tyr for the third.

The literal meaning of the name has often been accepted by modern sources as 'hail' or 'hagel' as in hailstones. The meaning of this rune is therefore quite clear: destructive elements of nature; severe weather. No one can control the weather so far as we know, although rumours abound on the Internet that major world governments are conducting research and experiments to this effect. Hagalaz is the rune of unavoidable unpleasantness outside individual control. Whatever is symbolized by Hagalaz when combined in a reading with other runes is, basically, inevitable. Hence this rune is strongly associated with Wyrd, and even with Órlog, the unalterable and inevitable law of the conditions of existence; the first primal layer in the Well of Wyrd which determines what shall become. The natural elemental destructive power of this rune cannot be harnessed by human beings. It is completely impersonal. It is the ultimate power of nature unveiled. The best one can do is to seek shelter and ride it out, and of course this can also be applied metaphorically when confronted with adverse happenings one cannot control, be it death, disease or the tax man! The lesson of Hagalaz is acceptance of that which cannot be changed, fortitude in the face of adversity and patience in the knowledge that the wheel soon turns again. This rune is strongly associated with early winter, particularly in November, when the weather is often worse than, for instance, in January. But as the Anglo-Saxon Runepoem says: 'Hail turns to water', and we all know water is the most vital substance of life itself. Hail will melt with a slight rise in temperature and becomes water, which is nutrition for the earth and all who live on her. Conversely, hail can turn to ice when the temperature changes the other way. Hagalaz, therefore, is a rune that embodies a force which is in itself potentially destructive but will change of its own accord given time. It either changes to Ice or more often to Water and fertilizes the earth. The change embodied in Hagalaz can go either way.

Germanic name: NAUTHIZ
Anglo-Saxon name: NEED
Old Norse name: NAUDR
Phonetic value: N
Traditional meaning: Need

Again no ambiguity here; the rune name speaks for itself. This is the rune of Need or necessity, again with the feeling of inevitability similar to the above Hagalaz rune. But need can be turned into an omen of help, if attended to early enough according to the Anglo-Saxon Runepoem. This is a rune which will warn and advise when recognized as such, when one encounters it either in a reading or in dreamscapes.

The first lesson of this rune is in practical down to earth terms; look at what is needed now! There is always the feeling of urgency about this rune. One of the most atavistic needs of humans was fire: without fire one died, period! The shape of Nauthiz represents two pieces of wood being rubbed together to generate fire. In these modern days, perhaps we cannot appreciate early man's need for fire. Fire as well as water is another vital element of life itself. The 'need-fire' was originally a ritual kindling of fire associated with various festivals such as Beltane, Midsummer, Yule and Samhain. It originates from a cult of fire-worship and evidence shows that this cult is older than the religion of the Aesir. The Aesir are the predominant clan of Gods in the North. They were patriarchal invaders who usurped and incorporated the earlier Vanir, the indigenous clan of Gods. The Aesir are the gods of social order, war, science, technology and communication. Their elements are Air and Fire. It is possible that this fire-worshipping cult is an overlap with the Celtic tradition, as around that time the tribes were sharing the same territory. Fire rituals were used for a variety of purposes, including sacrifice, healing and cleansing. In the need-fire ritual two fires were kindled a distance apart from each other by two chaste youngsters, one male and one female. Each made a fire by rubbing dry wood together until it caught light. Cattle were then driven between the two fires to ensure their fertility and health. (The custom of engaged couples leaping over a bonfire is a survival of this rite.) The need-fire was usually kindled in times of need such as dearth, drought and disease.

It is easily understandable why fire was held to be sacred, for the Northern climate is prone to extremes of cold, and our lands in the past were covered with dense forests where fire could easily become a destructive and deadly foe. The need for fire was balanced by the fear of fire. The Nauthiz rune also then has associations with an element as has Isa, the next rune in the Futhark.

Germanic name: ISA
Anglo-Saxon name: IS
Old Norse name: IS
Phonetic value: I
Traditional meaning: Ice

Here is the third rune of the second Aett. Isa, or Ice, is another elemental rune. Ice like hail is a variant of water. Ice is water in its densest frozen state. It is cold and slippery but it has its uses. For example, it preserves, and where would we be without our freezers!

Water is fluid; ice is solid and static. Isa therefore represents the principle of preservation and resistance to change. Isa is a necessary force whose controlling effect is essential in order to prevent random growth. Isa is static; it 'is'. Its function is to keep things as they are, to maintain whatsoever 'is'. On its own, it is an inert rune which merely preserves and conserves. Ice is inimical to life and hostile to the environment. It maintains its integrity, it is immobile and cannot change by itself; only when the opposite element of fire is brought into play can it generate 'steam'. Fire and Ice are, in the Northern tradition, in exactly the same intertwined relationship as Yang and Yin in the more well-known Taoist tradition, they are indispensable to each other and between them they create and maintain all existence, balancing each other perfectly. So far we have seen that Hagalaz is a so-called 'elemental' rune, hail being a state of water, Nauthiz we see clearly contains the element of fire and Isa, being ice, is also a state of water. The lesson of Isa is stability and maintaining one's integrity, and focus in a crisis situation. Psychologically, Isa represents the 'I' in the most mundane sense, and the capacity for personal survival through concentrated effort. Isa can be a great help in concentrating the will in a single-minded action. It is the rune of self-preservation and

self-containment, the positive aspect of which is our individualism and the ability to survive against all odds. The negative aspect can be self-centredness.

Germanic name: JERA ᛃ
Anglo-Saxon name: GER
Old Norse name: AR
Phonetic value: J or Y
Traditional meaning: year, harvest

That this rune is the fourth in the aett of Hagalaz and the twelfth in the Futhark is a good example of synchronicity, since there are twelve months in the year and twice twelve hours in a day. Also four is a third of twelve, as eight is a third of twenty-four.

It cannot be disputed that the order and numbering of the Futhark is a 'magical' act, and one of the highest order. We will get to magic later in the book though, for now we will examine the meaning of the Jera rune. The literal translation of Jera is year and this is the first indication that this rune has an important bearing on time and the divisions of time. This rune represents time itself. The shape of the rune is divided into two halves, clearly portraying two halves of a year circling around each other in perpetual swirling motion from light to darkness and back again. The Jera rune is associated, in particular, with the turning of the year at Yuletide, when the Sun returns, Yule being about the biggest festival of the North. It celebrates the return of the sun and the days lengthening gently, turning the wheel of the year until Midsummer's day, and so on in perpetual motion, spiralling upwards to the realm of the gods themselves. Jera is the rune of time and fruition, what comes around goes around, as the saying goes. Nowhere is that better portrayed than in the lessons of the Jera rune. Jera gives growth, there are mysteries which only time can teach: only experience, not hearsay will do. This is the rune of personal experience through time. Time itself, however, may not be what it once was.

Germanic name: EIHWAZ ᛇ
Anglo-Saxon name: EOH
Old Norse name: none
Phonetic value: E
Traditional meaning: Yew

This, the thirteenth rune in the Futhark, is named after a Tree, and not just any old tree.

Eihwaz represents the mother of all trees: Yggdrasil itself. This rune is associated with the world of nature, specifically trees. The Germanic tribes, like their Celtic neighbours, held trees in high regard, they in fact worshipped trees, or rather they conducted the services of worship to the gods in groves of trees. Only in later Scandinavia do we hear about temples or, more properly named, Hofs. The older Germanic tribes like the Druids, with whom they had far more in common than is known today, preferred a natural environment to conduct their spiritual and magical practices. The evergreen Yew tree was perceived as very sacred. Its wood was used for bows in hunting, and also for the crafting of rune staves. The wood is hard; the hardest wood to carve I have come across. The Yew tree is associated with both life and death, as it is an evergreen and a hardy tree it symbolizes longevity. At the same time, the berries and the firs are toxic, in fact a British Druid in the mid-1980s chose to end his life by eating a bowl of yew leaves. The same toxicity, when prepared properly by a qualified herbalist or chemist, can be used as a hallucinogenic, for shamanic initiatory purposes. Homeopathically, Taxus Baccata is a remedy to eliminate toxins from the body, especially residues from inoculations received in childhood.

It is the most holy tree in the Northern Tradition, the tree on which Odin was said to have hung for nine days and nine nights to received the 'Runes'. 'Runes' should be understood in this context as the 'Greater Mysteries' of life, death, evolution, ascension and transformation. These mysteries are contained in coded form in the Futhark runes as they have been handed down to us.

Germanic name: PERTHRO   ᛈ
Anglo-Saxon name: PEORTH
Old Norse name: none
Phonetic value: P
Traditional meaning: unknown

This is the rune everyone speculates about. The word Perthro has not been clearly identified with any of the known words in Germanic languages, either ancient or modern. There is no traditional and accepted meaning for this rune. I therefore follow everyone else and rely on my intuition to offer a provisional interpretation. To me this rune contains the mysteries of birth and rebirth. It seems a logical progression that, as the previous rune Eihwaz is connected with the mysteries of death, this one would be related to birth. The shape of the rune resembles a birth-giving position. Furthermore, I also associate this rune with the collective memory, the well of Mimir: memories of previous existences, ancestral memories, all can be retrieved from the Well of Mimir or the Akasha Records as it is also known in the esoteric body of lore. Destiny or 'wyrd' and that which one brings with one when entering life can also be perceived through this rune. Perthro can connect us with the 'unseen', the hidden knowledge.

Through Perthro one may perceive one's wyrd and be able to alter certain probabilities within that wyrd.

Germanic name: ALGIZ   ᛉ
Anglo-Saxon name: EOLH
Old Norse name: YR
Phonetic value: Z
Traditional meaning: protection

The traditional and accepted meaning of protection has been derived from the word Algiz, which most likely seems to have been related to 'alcis'. Alcis, according to Tacitus, was the name of the divine twins worshipped by Germanic people. Another form of the name of this rune is the Old Germanic word 'alhs' which means temple or sanctuary. Because all the magical accoutrements and ritual equipment were kept in the alhs, these sacred places of worship had to be strongly defended and protected magically.

This rune is the best for defence and protection of the individual as well as the group. The sign itself looks like a splayed hand, and is reminiscent of Tyr's hand, which he sacrificed in order to bind Fenrir the wolf. This rune can be seen to have two forms, upright and inverted. It has been a historical custom in Germany to use Algiz runes on gravestones in the following manner:

Date of birth: ᛉ   Date of death: ᛣ

The upright form is a classical pose of an invocation or supplication to the gods, especially to ask for protection and guidance. It is the most prominent rune to be used in devotional worship, as it both protects the human from undesirable astral or mundane interference and acts as a channel or conduit to transmit the god force and allow safe communication to occur.

Germanic name: SOWULO 〉
Anglo-Saxon name: SIGIL
Old Norse name: SOL
Phonetic value: S
Traditional meaning: Sun

The sun, the life-giving force — in the human body the heart — represents the seat of the soul, the higher potential. The guiding path of solar initiation.

Our ancestors depended very much on the power of the sun, so much so that it has been preserved as a rune name, whereas there is no equivalent name for the moon preserved in the Futhark. However, one important contradiction with present-day pagan traditions is that the sun was regarded as being of the female polarity. This is in contrast to popular paganism, derived from the Greek tradition and expressed in modern Wicca and the Western Mysteries, where the sun is seen as masculine. In modern German the grammatical gender of 'die Sonne' is feminine. Both interpretations, of course, are as valid as each other, it is all a matter of perspective and relative to the aeon. Male or female, we know the sun gives growth and healing. Our ancestors navigated their ships by the position of the sun in daytime, and by the Pole Star at night. Sowulo then represents the clear light of day.

There is nevertheless a destructive element in this rune. It is shaped like a lightning flash. Like lightning, Sowulo strikes suddenly, sweeping aside everything in its way, usually in order to prepare for something better (just as when the atmosphere exudes negative ions following a thunderstorm).

Germanic name: TEIWAZ ↑
Anglo-Saxon name: TYR
Old Norse name: TYR
Phonetic value: T
Traditional meaning: the god Tyr

The third Aett is called the Aett of Tyr as is the name of the first rune of this Aett. Tyr is one of the oldest gods, known to have been 'top dog' before Odin took over. This we know from various historical writings, although the Norse pantheon was actually a lot more 'egalitarian' to use a modern word. The hierarchy of the gods is largely due to Snorri Sturluson, a classical scholar, who, thank the gods, recorded most of the material and modelled the Norse pantheon on the Greek one. Tyr, despite his relegation by Sturluson to a less significant role as a minor son of Odin, is still one of the most important gods.

Whereas the Ansuz rune refers to Odin, Tyr is actually named. The Tyr rune is a warrior's rune. It is invoked and inscribed on weapons to ensure victory. Tyr represent right course of action in a military conflict. It cannot be denied that, however undesirable, warfare and conflicts are part of human evolution. Tyr is the god of natural justice, hence the Tyr rune is often of great help in assuring a favourable outcome in litigations, legal warfare. Tyr also is the god of the 'Thing', a folk assembly where disputes could be arbitrated. Tyr, therefore, would be an excellent god for judges, whereas Odin's rune Ansuz would be a good rune for solicitors! The Tyr rune stands for bravery, honesty and even-handedness. The name Tir is also the Old Persian name for the Pole Star by which our ancestors navigated at night. Like the Sowulo rune, the Tyr rune also is a guiding principle.

Tyr was the original Skyfather. The shape of the Teiwaz rune resembles Irminsul, which is a symbolic representation of Yggdrasil as the cosmic axis.

Germanic name: BERKANA   ᛒ
Anglo-Saxon name: BEORC
Old Norse name: BJARKAN
Phonetic value: B
Traditional meaning: birch

In the majority of the Germanic languages this rune name translates as 'birch'. However, the Anglo-Saxons translated it as 'poplar'. The birch is a very sacred tree: due to its resilient nature it was the first tree to reforest our lands after the Ice Age. As such this rune represent all trees and plantlife.

First and foremost this is a goddess-orientated rune. Pictographically, it resembles a pair of breasts when viewed from above. This rune especially relates to the goddess Holda, in southern Germany known as Berchta, who is the patron of children and domestic animals, especially dogs. She resides in the underworld; there she has a beautiful garden where the young children who die in infancy are said to go, as do dogs.

The Berkana rune, in particular, refers to the processes of gestation and birth. Perthro looks like an opened-up Berkana, which suggests that what remains a hidden promise in Berkana will be brought into the open by Perthro. For this reason Berkana is also associated with secrecy and containment. Another goddess who co-rules Berkana is Frigg, the goddess of silence. Berkana is a rune of healing, recuperation, rejuvenation and purification. In Scandinavia, birch twigs are used for scourging after a sauna to stimulate the circulation and detoxify the blood. It stands to reason that there was originally a spiritual element involved in this practice.

The Berkana rune is very feminine and in this respect is a great healing rune for female problems. It can be used for healing and alleviating both menstrual and menopausal symptoms. Apart from all the life-giving aspects, there is a connection with death as well: the goddess Berchta is known in Germany as 'the White Lady' and used to appear as a ghost, according to folklore, whenever a person of royal birth was to die.

Germanic name: EHWAZ   M
Anglo-Saxon name: EOH
Old Norse name: none
Phonetic value: E
Traditional meaning: horse

The Ehwaz rune means Horse, so if the previous rune represents trees and plants this one represents animals, in particular the Horse. Horses have always been sacred, they are second only to humans in value of sacrifice. I think that for the slaying of a horse 'were gild' (literally 'man money' which was paid in compensation to the victim's family for the killing of a man or woman in a 'fair fight') was due as for humans. Man's life often depended on the Horse. My first impression of this rune was that it represented a mare. Unlike most warriors, who rode stallions, priests of the old faith of the Aesir rode mares.

Metaphorically, Ehwaz also represents the physical vehicle and may be incorporated in a healing working. On a deeper level, the Ehwaz rune represents the persona, which is used to relate to the external world through one's own emotional attitudes. The horse is also a power animal and shamanically often gives assistance in travelling to other realms. In dreams the horse represents the astral body.

Ehwaz, moreover, emphatically relates to Sleipnir, Odin's eight-legged horse. In the continental Germanic tradition

Wodan, especially, was worshipped as the god of horses, although in Scandinavia this was attributed to Frey. Hence there is still a taboo about eating horse flesh, especially in England. Even in recent times rumours have been circulated about the existence of a society of 'horse whisperers' who were a magical fraternity. This may well be a vestige of one of the horse-cults of olden days.

Horses where used for magic, in a variety of ways, one of which was to use a horse's head on a 'nithing pole', which had insults and curses written upon it. The nithing pole was used to curse — to either destroy or drive out an opponent. The night-mare is another variant of malicious magic involving horses, which consists of shaping the astral body into a horse and hunting down and attacking your enemy.

Lastly, Ehwaz is also the rune most associated with marriages or other forms of partnership, and of course this includes the part-nership between a horse and its rider. Horses are stronger than us, they cannot be forced, only persuaded to do our will. Therefore this rune is an important asset to any form of co-operation.

Germanic name: MANNAZ ᛗ
Anglo-Saxon name: MAN
Old Norse name: MADR
Phonetic value: M
Traditional meaning: man

Whereas the previous two runes referred to plant and animal kingdoms respectively, this, the third rune of the third Aett, refers to 'man'.

Here is another example of the logic and reason behind the sequence of the runes in the futhark. The previous rune, Ehwaz, was mainly related to animals, in particular to horses. The Mannaz rune is similar in shape to the Ehwaz rune, which makes sense as man is after all an animal with above-average intelligence. It goes without saying that 'man' means *homo sapiens*. In the Anglo-Saxon branch of the Germanic language, 'man' denoted not just the male section of the population. The words for men and women were 'weapmen' and 'weavemen' respectively; clearly the former means men with weapons, and the latter translates literally as 'men who weave', ie women.

This rune not only means 'man' or 'mankind', it is also the name of mankind's ancestor and progenitor. In the Continental Germanic tradition Mannaz, who is mentioned by Tacitus as the progenitor of the Germanic people, was the son of Tuisco, who was Earth-born. Tuisco is an older form of Tyr; thus Mannaz was a tribal ancestor god. He, in turn, had three sons: Ingvio, whose name appeared in the Inguz rune, Irmio and Istio. These are also the names of the three main branches of the West Germanic tribes. He corresponds to Heimdallr who, according to the 'Rigsthula', one of the poems of the Eddas, is the progenitor of the three classes. This poem describes how HeimdallR sets off on a journey to Midgard and is the guest of three married couples in turn. He spends the night with each couple, sleeping between the man and the woman; later all three women give birth to his sons. The Mannaz rune signifies cooperation between people sharing the same environment for the benefit of the whole of the tribe, or community. Mannaz is a double Wunjo, and we have already discussed that Wunjo is the rune of the clan. Mannaz expresses the development of man's intellectual powers, and of his awareness as co-creator of Nature. Initially primitive and subject to the environment, man, via money, now unfortunately has too much control over Nature and is destroying his environment. However; it seems that the Mother has had enough! Shame about the plants and animals though.

Germanic name: LAGUZ
Anglo-Saxon name: LAGU
Old Norse name: LOGR
Phonetic value: L
Traditional meaning: lake or water

Laguz translates as the sea, or a large lake, as some of the Germanic tribes lived near the sea and some more inland. The goddess I associate with this rune is Nerthus. She is not much heard of in the Norse mythos but in Germany and Holland, according to the Roman historian Tacitus, she was once held in a similar regard as Isis.

This rune, therefore, is predominantly feminine. The goddess Nerthus is probably the oldest goddess known from Germanic sources and she was worshipped on an island in a lake, possibly in Frisia. She was supposed to bestow blessings wherever she visited. Once a year, everyone laid down their weapons while her wagon was ritually driven around the mainland; a remnant of this was observed in medieval Holland, where a decorated ship was used in processions. Laguz was also probably connected with the custom of ship-burial and Odin was the Ferryman. In Holland we know of a native goddess named Nehelennia. Statues of her dating from the first century have been found in Walcheren, one of the islands of the Dutch province of Zealand. She is portrayed with a dog and a basket of apples, and she was sometimes described as holding a horn of plenty. She may be a localized form of Nerthus. Laguz represents the waters of life without which we would not be, but also of death as many, many of our people, especially from the Lowlands, lost their lives at sea.

Laguz is nevertheless one of the runes of healing and initiation. In many traditions water is used to 'initiate' a newborn into the clan. In modern magical work water plays a major role.

Laguz, according to some German writers, also means love. There is some truth in this interpretation, for if Laguz symbolizes the waters of life, it may represent the forces of mutual attraction called 'love'. In fact, the shape of Laguz is that of a half-Ehwaz, the rune of partnerships and marriages.

Germanic name: INGUZ ◇
Anglo-Saxon name: ING
Old Norse name: none
Phonetic value: NG
Traditional meaning: the god Yngvi — Frey

The name of this rune is the oldest name of the Scandinavian fertility god Yngvi, or Frey. Nothing is known of him from Germanic source material, but as his name appears in the common Germanic Futhark, the oldest recorded rune row, he most certainly was known. His name has been preserved in the Anglo-Saxon Runepoem. Frey was especially important among the Danes: he was a god of peace and plenty. Out of all the gods he is probably the nicest one for humans to follow. Having said that, I stick with Odin, though! The Inguz rune is very much associated with agriculture, as Frey is not just a god of male and animal fertility he is also the god of vegetation and food, a far more civilized character than 'Old Pan', for example. However, he is definitely also the god of male sexuality, and that includes homosexuality. Although frowned upon in the Viking Age, it wasn't actually illegal and priests of Frey in Sweden engaged in cross-dressing and dancing, and were involved in Seith, a magical discipline usually preserved for women.

But all this does not exclude the notion that Frey is one of the gods of procreation. If we take the Anglo-Saxon form of Inguz and duplicate it a few times: ⌇ we can see that it has a remarkable similarity to a double helix, the shape of the DNA chain.

Inguz is the carrier of genetic material and confers upon the individual inherited characteristics of his or her ancestors.

Inguz is closely related to Kenaz and Jera and can be seen as a progression of these runes. We can view Kenaz as either the male or female half of a polarity, depending on the gender of the person who is working with it. With Jera we see two similar shapes circling around each other. In the shape of the Inguz rune we find both halves joined and integrated, symbolizing completion, totality and fulfilment.

Germanic name: OTHALA ᛟ
Anglo-Saxon name: ETHEL
Old Norse name: none
Phonetic value: O
Traditional meaning: inherited land

Inherited land and the family estate are the meanings associated to this, the seventh rune of the third Aett, and quite rightly so. But there is more to this when we examine the literal meaning of the word Othala. The oldest literal meaning is 'noble'. It is directly related to the Anglo-Saxon word 'atheling', meaning 'prince' or 'noble'.

The god who is most obviously related to this rune is Odin. The shape of Othala is a combination of Inguz and Gebo, and Othala can be interpreted as the 'gift of Ing', which probably explains why Othala has been related to the concept of inheritance by some modern commentators. By comparing the concept of inheritance to the Inguz rune, the previous rune in the futhark, it can be established that it is genetic material that is being inherited. Genetic material contains the hamingja of the ancestral stream into which one is born, and this was even more so in the case of noble birth. In the Germanic tribal system the king was believed to be descended from the gods, usually from

Odin but sometimes from Frey or Tyr. Furthermore, the king was seen as the bearer of the hamingja of his people. It was customary that when a king ran out of luck and could no longer guarantee prosperity and the power of fertility for the land, he was sacrificed. And the land as well as the hamingja or 'luck' of the country or tribe was inherited by the successor. The son became the next king if he was fit for the office; if not, another member of the royal family would succeed to the throne. Therefore, the choice of the king's wife was considered especially important in light of the belief that the offspring would be the next to bear the hamingja of the people and would inherit the king's 'luck' and vital abilities, such as courage and wisdom.

Germanic name: DAGAZ ᛞ
Anglo-Saxon name: DAEG
Old Norse name: none
Phonetic value: D
Traditional and literally meaning: Day

All these words are derived from the name Dagaz. The associations of this rune are primarily with either the dawning of the new day or else with the mid-point of the day, when the Sun is at its zenith, at noon. It is remarkable that the Germanic people did not have a rune for 'night' but only for 'day', even though they counted their days by nights, as in English. This is even preserved today in the expression 'a fortnight [fourteen night] from now'. Likewise, they have a rune for 'sun' but not for 'moon'.

Dagaz is assigned to the controlling power of Loki and, to a certain extent, HeimdallR, Loki's counterpart. The 'hidden' invisible transforming power of Dagaz is indisputable; Odin. Dagaz is a hidden doorway to other worlds, even other planets and universes.

The shape of the rune resembles a lemniscate, the symbol of infinity; it also resembles a Moebius strip, a symbol of time-lessness and unlimited possibilities, and as such Dagaz takes us beyond time and space. This is, in my opinion, correctly assigned as the last rune of the futhark as it completes a cycle, which in actual fact is a spiral pathway of evolution, continuing on the next level. Dagaz is above and beyond all levels of being. It is both being and non-being and stands for the supreme mystery of existence. Dagaz operates between light and darkness, mediating in both directions but partaking of neither. Dagaz synthesizes, transmutes and dissolves all opposing polarities. This rune can transform consciousness, and it is the most appropriate rune for the purpose of initiation.

COMMON GERMANIC FUTHARK

Rune	Name	Traditional meaning	Letter	Meaning
	Fehu	cattle	F	Money, wealth, hamingja
	Uruz	aurochs	U	Health, strength, endurance
	Thurisaz	giant	Th	Conflicts, annoyance, strife
	Ansuz	god	A	Communication, inspiration, ancestors
	Raido	riding	R	Control, direction, right or wrong advice
	Kenaz	torch	K	Knowledge, learning and teaching
	Gebo	gift	G	to give, to receive, to share or agree
	Wunjo	joy	W	Joy, perfected Will
	Hagalaz	hail	H	Disruption, unresolved matters, the past
	Nauthiz	need	N	Necessity, friction, warnings
	Isa	ice	I	Restrictions, delay
	Jera	year/harvest	J/Y	Harvest, year, seasonal/karmic returns, the Earth
	Eihwaz	yew	EI	Yew, Tree of Life/Death, Yggdrasil
	Perthro	fruit(?)	P	Womb, space, Well of Urd/Mimir
	Algiz	protection	Z	Protection, defence, wardings
	Sowulo	sun	S	Life-force, clarity, understanding
	Teiwaz	Tyr	T	Spiritual Warrior, Justice, Thing
	Berkana	birch	B	Great Mother, nurturing, protecting children
	Ehwaz	horse	E	The various bodies as vehicles for travel and movement
	Mannaz	human	M	Intelligence, reason, Law
	Laguz	water	L	Feeling, intuition, empathy
	Inguz	Yngvi/Frey	Ng	Fruitfulness, peace and plenty
	Othala	inherited land	O	Genetic, cultural and spiritual inheritance
	Dagaz	day	D	Day, dawn, enlightenment

DEEPER MYSTERIES OF THE RUNES

I n this chapter we will look further into the runes, exploring how they may be used to improve people's lives, circumstances and understanding.

FIRST AETT

We start, once again, with the first aett, which is the aett of creation of all beings: gods, giants, humans, elves, dwarfs and all else besides. The runes of this aett set things in motion; they are the origins of being. For the purpose of divination, therefore, the runes of this aett often express the basic principles of life — such as money, health, conflict, intelligence, control, knowledge, balance and pleasure.

FEHU

Fehu, on the basic level as we have seen, represents money or wealth. Money is only the simplest, most mundane meaning of this rune, but it is worth dwelling on the concept. Money does not arise from nothing, nor does it last indefinitely. It is either earned or inherited; then we spend or invest it. Thus it remains constantly in motion (otherwise it quickly loses its value). The esoteric equivalent of money is therefore energy; energy of a kind that can be harnessed and used. A higher meaning still, therefore, is the vital force of life, the initial spark, creative and mobile, which guides our actions. Bringing all three levels together, then, the Fehu rune serves as the key to the personal powerbase from which practical goals — such as, earning money — can be attained.

The inner power, of which money is only a pale, unreliable shadow is the 'hamingja' or personal power. Strong hamingja enables one to achieve one's objectives — including, for example, making money. Fehu can endow you with this ability if the objective itself is within your 'wyrd'. Hamingja as well as wyrd (which corresponds, very roughly, to the Eastern concept of 'karma') can be passed on from one generation to the next. The store of hamingja you are born with may be added to or subtracted from by acts of honour or lack thereof. The hamingja is thus a storehouse of 'luck' on the Inner Planes. However, there are people who inherit good luck and still manage to screw up and others who inherit bad luck and succeed. In everyday life the greatest influence on your hamingja is the esteem in which you are held by your peers, ie your reputation — and of course that includes self-esteem, which is often negatively programmed by upbringing. Thoughts, too, are a form of energy; therefore, negative thoughts can create negative thought-forms and positive thoughts can create positive thought-forms. The ultimate exercise of power using the hamingja is to be aware of this, and consciously participate in creating your own reality — not allowing others, usually with their own agendas, to 'program' this for you.

The Fehu rune is the first and most powerful rune to call upon for help in a crisis situation. It functions a bit like a rescue remedy, infusing you with the necessary power — physical, psychic or magical — to deal with any problems on the spot.

The Fehu rune can be used to increase your hamingja and access this creative power source. Fehu can be used to give the impetus to any intent, backed up by an act of will. It can be used in conjunction with other runes to forcefully break down negative programming and 'turn your luck'. However, it usually brings the kind of 'lucky break' that turns hard work and patient effort into success — so don't count on it helping you to win the lottery!

FEHU

Spiritual aspect: Life force
Emotional or psychological aspect: self-confidence
Negative aspect: fear of failure

AUROCHS OR URUZ

The magical power of Uruz is health, vitality and strength on all levels. Whereas Fehu can be invoked to energize and initiate an operation, Uruz will enable you to shape and maintain it. Fehu is dynamic force, while Uruz is enduring form. Thus Uruz relates primarily to health, which is, of course, much more important than money or wealth. If you are healthy you can work all hours of the day to create wealth, but no amount of wealth can create health.

As Fehu is the rune of the power of the hamingja, or inner potential, Uruz is the rune of the power to manifest your will in the real world of matter. Fehu, properly invoked, will give you an inspiration to improve your financial circumstances, whereas Uruz will, if properly invoked, empower you with the determination and persistence to carry the idea out into the world.

So many original and inspirational ideas keep floating in the air until their power is dissipated. The idea loses its original attraction and is dismissed or forgotten. Uruz embodies our capacity to keep the initiative going; it is the primary rune to be invoked for physical energy and stamina, so that we can persist at times when this is necessary. However, the energy of Uruz is raw and primitive and has to be moderated by the mind's understanding. It cannot merely be invoked and let loose. The correct application of this force, when controlled by personal discipline, makes us both resourceful and persistent. Uruz is the will to live, the primal impulse to be and to become.

In German and Dutch, 'ur' means 'primal' or 'ancient'. This appears in the name of one of the Norns, Urd, who embodies the great web of past reality, established laws and causes, deep-laid patterns and powerful trends, which underlie, inform and shape the present. Uruz is very much associated with growth, evolution and, through conflict and challenge, the overcoming of obstacles, the force to assert oneself and to assert one's right to one's own space. This interpretation is also applicable on the psychological level.

Uruz is a powerful healing rune, in combination with other runes which we will discuss later. It can bestow rejuvenation and regeneration of physical health. A simple and effective way to enhance one's strength at a moment when it is needed is to take a glass of clean water and, with the index and middle fingers, trace an Uruz rune over the surface of the water. Visualize the rune in brilliant red, and chant the rune name in a deep voice, letting the power of the rune charge the water. Maintain the visualization for several seconds and then drink the water. Another method would be to chant Uruz over a hot, herbal bath nine times, before getting in and feeling your exhaustion being washed away. (Please note: I do not recommend drinking the bathwater afterwards!)

I have come to believe that the higher form of the power of Uruz is akin to what is known in the east as Chi. Invoke the power of Uruz into your hands until they feel as if they glow,

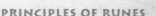

and with this force field you can heal people and animals and charge objects of power, especially in combination with other runes.

URUZ
spiritual aspect: healing and rejuvenation
emotional or psychological aspect: moral strength
negative aspect: uncontrolled rage

THURISAZ OR THORN

Thurisaz, the most dangerous rune in the futhark, can destroy as well as protect; its function is to attack, defend or protect one from hostile forces. It is a battle rune, a rune of war and conflict. Ideally, we would live in a world of unconditional love, positive regard and universal peace, but unfortunately, that's going to take some time. In the meantime, one has to look after oneself and one's kin. This rune is as active as a power cable. The energy it can wield is enormous, and its use should not be taken lightly. The only time I have used Thurisaz in anger was when my life was clearly in danger. Suffice to say, it worked; I'm in no hurry to use it again in this way: but the rune does have other, less drastic uses.

Thurisaz is the rune of ultimate physical fighting force and as such it has been attributed to both Thor and the giants. The power contained in this rune is the power of Thor's hammer, Mjolnir. Thor never slays innocent human beings, only certain destructive forces represented as giants. Mjolnir's prime function is to ward or protect, and it is here we find the best side of the rune Thurisaz. It is equally strong to protect and defend as it is to attack; a circle of eight fiery red Thurisaz runes on the eight quarters will keep everything at bay. More than that, it acts as an automatic missile and throws everything back at the sender, with accelerated force, so there is no need to attack first. A good strategy is: never start a fight if you can avoid it, but be prepared to finish one, when it is needful!

Mjolnir is not only associated with conflict, strength and protection, but also with hallowing and blessing. Thor himself has a fertility aspect, bringing vitality to the fields through lightning and rain. There is evidence to suggest that the hammer was used to hallow the bride in Heathen wedding ceremonies. All this suggests that the Thurisaz rune may have a gentler, healing aspect. In this connection, the phallic shape of the rune suggests an association with male sexual prowess. Here, the energy of Thurisaz may be expressed in a way that is self-assertive and co-operative rather than aggressive and hostile. When invoking Thurisaz for this purpose, it is important to concentrate on these non-aggressive aspects; otherwise, you will run the risk of linking heightened sexual energy with hostility, conflict and violence. Needless to say, this would be a grave mistake, with potentially harmful consequences for all concerned.

THURISAZ
spiritual aspect: courage, self-empowerment
emotional or psychological aspect: assertiveness, male sexuality
negative aspect: disease, explosive violence

ANSUZ

This rune is associated with the higher mental abilities: thinking, connecting and communicating. The name Ansuz can mean both 'god' and 'ancestors'. In Asatru, we take this god to be Odin, but theoretically it could mean any deity or divine intelligence. It is specifically the rune of intellectual learning, understanding, abstract thought processes and the ability to

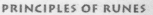

communicate these in concrete terms. Also, language skills: both the ability with words, to write, to speak, as well as the language of symbols. Ansuz is one of the runes of leadership, particularly in the sense of teaching and spiritual instruction. Human ancestors and gods alike were thought of as Elders: that is, wiser, older kinfolk from whom advice is sought. By meditating on or chanting the Ansuz rune, we can open channels of inspiration previously inaccessible. Out of all the runes, it is the most meaningful for me as it represents to me the force of Odin himself, the highest source of consciousness and awareness.

Ansuz can open hidden 'doorways' through which we can obtain occult knowledge about the ancestors, tapping into the reservoirs of ancestral knowledge that remain on the Inner Planes. The modern practice of channelling, which in reality is a practice as old as humankind, can be developed safely by means of invoking the Ansuz rune, especially so-called conscious channelling, where one does not surrender consciousness but merges with a greater mind in order to transmit knowledge.

ANSUZ

spiritual aspect: higher consciousness, mental stability
emotional or psychological aspect: knowledge of self and discipline
negative aspect: neurosis, compulsive lying

RAIDO

The Raido rune represents the journey of life, the direction in which one travels and the amount of control one may exert over the direction. This holds true on several levels, from the physical, mundane progress of our lives from childhood to adulthood and old age, to the spiritual and magical journeys we may also undertake. Such paths of initiation and evolution may be taken consciously, in co-operation with and in service of higher forces; or unconsciously, subject to the decree of the Norns, the Nordic weavers of fate. The Norns are the three goddesses of fate, portrayed in Macbeth as the wyrd sisters. Their names are Urd, Verdandi and Skuld. Urd represents 'that which is and has been'; Verdandi represents 'that which is becoming', and Skuld represents 'that which should come about'. In the most simple terms they are seen as past, present and future.

The magical and psychological significance of this rune relates to the ability to move within one's natural limits and, consequently, to become aware of what these limits are. Realistic assessment of parameters given in life is essential, practical knowledge. The rune also refers to the power of making a conscious decision and the discipline to carry it out. Raido can also be used in a magical working to establish control over one's own circumstances, to put things in order and make them subject to one's will, in accordance with wyrd.

Inherent in Raido are the ideas of freedom and moral responsibility to the Self (even if this conflicts with the norms prevailing in the present-day social structure), as well as the knowledge of right and wrong in the personal, developed conscience and the courage to act accordingly. Thus, working with the force of Raido means to be in charge of your own path in life; to keep your own counsel; to ride, not to be ridden; as far as is possible, to be master of your own circumstances; to extend gradually the degree of control that you exercise over these circumstances; and finally to make a conscious choice of the direction you wish to follow. How much of yourself is being ridden, so to speak, depends upon your magical control, that is, conscious control over the ego as a rider controls his horse, or a driver his vehicle.

---

spiritual aspect: ethical conduct
emotional or psychological aspect: control issues
negative aspect: control freak, dictator, hypocrite

KENAZ

Kenaz, mostly interpreted as 'torch' is the rune which lights your path. It exposes, enlightens and informs. This rune is also associated with intellectual abilities, especially the ability to recognize and learn. Kenaz will make the invisible visible; it dispels darkness and ignorance. Thus, for example, it can sometimes be helpful when inquiring into others' possible hidden or ulterior motives. The power of this rune can be invoked, just like other runes, by repetitive chanting of its name while visualizing its form as an imprint in brilliant white light before the 'third eye' (roughly, just above the bridge of your nose). Invoking Kenaz in this way, just before going to sleep, may help to illuminate an issue which was difficult to understand at first, and can confer a bright idea or a solution — particularly if you are in the habit of keeping a dream-diary.

Kenaz represents the light within; confidence in the knowledge that one is descended from the gods, kings and tribal chieftains; and with this, the responsibility to hand over the torch to the next generation, or else to share its light by teaching. On a psychological level, the attributes of Kenaz are clarity of thought, insight, consciousness of the self, inborn or hereditary knowledge, confidence and trust in one's own intuition, and finally, concentration and determined effort. Kenaz and Raido together can give you recognition of re-occurring patterns in your life and relationships.

spiritual aspect: knowledge from within, intuition, enlightenment

emotional or psychological aspect: self-knowledge, self-awareness

negative aspect: ignorance, arrogance

GEBO

This is the rune of giving in all its forms, and fair exchange. The higher aspect of the Gebo rune is the unconditional giving of self to Self, that is, to the gods from whence we came and to whom everything ultimately will return. The soul on its journey through life, gaining knowledge, is always homeward bound to return the gift; those gifts of life and consciousness which are the gifts of the gods to man. In Norse mythology, the story is told of how the three gods Odin, Hoenir and Lodur encounter two trees, Ask (male tree) and Embla (female tree). Each of the gods gives a gift of life, by which Ask becomes the first man and Embla the first woman.

The Gebo rune also implies the gifts that man gives to the gods in return. Man's gifts to the gods include service, loyalty and dedication to whatever is conceived to be 'the gods'. In this sense Gebo may imply the voluntary sacrifice of one's resources, time and energy to whatever one holds sacred, without an expectation of reward other than the development of one's own potential. In extreme cases, this gift is the supreme sacrifice. On the highest level, the gift transcends both giver and receiver, thus implying the synthesis of gift, giver and receiver of the gift in a unity; the result is the dissolving of barriers between all, mystical union through complete giving, and the surrender of one's ego to the divine consciousness, which is also known as the higher Self.

48

GEBO

spiritual aspect: integration of complimentary opposites
emotional or psychological aspect: balancing opposite facets
of the self
negative aspect: unbalanced behaviour, dishonesty

WUNJO

This is the rune of joy and fulfilment of desires, optimism and
contentment. Wunjo embodies the power of the will. Odin, who
controls the power of this rune, has three aspects: Odin, Vili and
Ve. Odin corresponds to Ansuz, Willi to Wunjo and We or Ve to
Othala, as we shall see. The name Vili, in Germanic Wili, fits the
concept of the magical application of the Wunjo rune and the art
of correct wishing, or in other words, the use of the power of the
magical will. Since all magic is fundamentally an act of will, we
see that this rune can be extremely useful in realizing one's
goals, whatever these may be. It combines very well with Raido
in that Raido operates as a means of controlling and directing
the will symbolized by Wunjo. Wunjo is excellent for group
bonding and sharing of ideals; it generates harmony and coop-
erative effort, a togetherness of like-minded people. Wunjo
especially is the rune for genuine friendship and comradeship.

From an esoteric and spiritual point of view, Wunjo can mean
joy when it is combined with Gebo, which symbolizes the gift
of one's own will to the gods, and in particular the alignment of
one's own individual will with the will of the god or goddess
one serves.

WUNJO

spiritual aspect: complete harmony with everything
emotional or psychological aspect: happiness, optimism
negative aspect: failure, misery, loneliness

The second aett introduces forces outside human control, such as the Norns, Time, Wyrd/orlog, multidimensional space, higher spiritual issues and initiation. This is the aett of development of consciousness and magic, psychological growth and personal evolution.

HAGALAZ

Hagalaz is the rune of the hidden realms of the past and the dead. Goddesses associated with the very dark female rune are Hella, Holda and Urd. Hagalaz can be used as a doorway to the past; your personal past within this lifetime where one may inquire about early environmental conditions, and also the transpersonal past to obtain information about previous lives. This is also one of the runes that may be used to call upon and communicate with the dead. This rune gives access to the 'underworld' or, in the Northern tradition, Hella's Halls. The realm of Hel is the equivalent of the shamanic underworld, and can be reached by shamanic means by travelling while in altered states of consciousness.

Hagalaz contains a lot of dark feminine power, and has a strong connection with negative witchcraft and destructive female magic. The first witch known in our mythology is a lady called Gullveig. Like Hella, she represents the dark aspect of the Goddess. Gullveig, we are told, introduced to Valhalla the lust for gold and thus corrupted the inhabitants of Asgard, so that Odin himself had to put a stop to it. She was burned three times and from this process, the Norns arose; the first being Urd, the eldest, who guards the past.

There is an alternative form of this rune which is very protective and is especially used to provide defence against bad weather. For this purpose it used to be displayed over doorways or on top of the house or farm. The protective aspect of Hagalaz, or Hail, is mostly referred to as 'heil', which can be used as both a blessing and a greeting. This form of the rune was particularly used as a marriage blessing and, as one can see, the shape of this rune looks like the two forms of the Algiz rune intertwined, indicating the union between the male and the female form of Algiz: ✕ This also resembles a snowflake: snow is one of the prime elements of the Goddess Holda; in winter she shakes her bed and it snows. Also, when the six points are joined together with a line it forms a hexagon, the molecular shape of carbon, the stuff of life itself in matter. Perhaps this rune is representative of the creation of the material world Midgard.

HAGALAZ

spiritual aspect: confers ability to learn from the past
emotional or psychological aspect: acceptance of past mistakes of self and others, letting go
negative aspect: victim consciousness, blaming others, obsession with the past

NAUTHIZ

Nauthiz, the need-rune, embodies the power by which friction and resistance generate creative energy. Need-fire used to be made by the friction between two pieces of wood. Likewise, progress and growth are often generated by friction, literally or metaphorically; for example, the friction between a growing adolescent and his or her elders. The need to achieve spurs creativity; as the saying goes, necessity is the mother of invention.

Need is usually triggered by distress. Nauthiz, therefore, often has a positive or negative connection with Fehu, for whatever the cause is of the distress, the necessity to act is ultimately a force of growth, albeit often unpleasant. In short, the Need rune kicks ass! It generates action and, by inference, change. Without the counterforce of Nauthiz, life would be a lot more static and growth would be at a much slower rate. Nauthiz, however, is a natural force outside the individual's control. One can work with it, one can work around it, one can magically use it, but one cannot ignore it!

As we have seen, Hagalaz represents, among other things, the forces of the past. Nauthiz can teach us how these forces can still exert their effect on us in the present, as the present is a continuation of the past and the past is really an incorporated part of the present. There is no sharp definition between the two, they overlap. Nauthiz can then endow us with insight and motivation to heal from our past, to extract the lessons from our and others' errors, then to get out of the blame-game and create something constructive using the power of the Nauthiz rune to build strength of character. In the words of Nietzsche, 'that which does not destroy me makes me stronger'! To grow in spite of opposition, resistance and constraint, we must simply become aware of what is needed — and do it.

NAUTHIZ

spiritual aspect: a generating force for the greater good and the long term

emotional or psychological aspect: confers the ability to recognize one's needs and cater for them

negative aspect: guilt, anxiety, neurosis, moral cowardice

ISA

This is one of the more enigmatic runes in the futhark: Isa, Ice. This rune is unyielding like the element after which it is named! The Isa rune has no glamour, yet although it is smooth and

slippery according to the Anglo-Saxon Runepoem, it shows itself as it is. Thus, the Isa rune is the rune of the Ego and the harsh reality of life. Ice is water in its densest frozen state. Ice is the complimentary opposite of Fire, and these two elements create and maintain all life. Water is fluid; ice is solid and static. Isa therefore represents the principle of preservation and resistance to change, and in this it maintains its own integrity.

Ice is inimical to life and hostile to the environment. Nevertheless, our ancestors saw it as a challenge, and not only succeeded in the struggle for survival in unfavourable conditions, but were also spurred on by Isa to evolve at a faster rate. Isa, however, often functions as a force of inertia, a block, psychological or otherwise. Working with one of the gentler runes of fire such as Kenaz or Sowulo can gradually dissolve blockages of this nature. Sometimes, this inertia is a good thing, though. Isa may make one slow down and re-evaluate one's position, and as such Isa can confer a clarity of sight and an objectivity devoid of emotion, in which the real solutions to your problems are revealed. Isa, therefore, has a recuperative ability; slow down, take stock and slowly proceed. Rest and regeneration are the positive aspects of this rune.

ISA

spiritual aspect: calming, reflective influence
emotional or psychological aspect: stability, conservation, integrity
negative aspect: gross materialism, greed

JERA

This rune expresses the mystery of time and cyclical recurrences, the natural cycle of the year and the turning of the wheel. The Jera rune furthermore is representative of the

Greater Cycles of Cosmic origin, for instance, the astronomical precession of the equinox. All these cycles are in fact spirals, through time; although they seem to be recurring in exactly the same way over longer periods of time, they are not mere repetitions.

A repetitive shape of the Jera rune can resemble the spiral arm of the galaxy of which our solar system is a part. All re-occurring cycles of time such as seasonal, astrological and astro-nomical are contained within the mysteries of the Jera rune, as is the turning of the Earth itself. I would therefore suggest that this rune is very much connected with Earth mysteries, the weather and the ecology of the planet. Others as well as myself have pointed out that the Jera rune has the secondary meaning of 'harvest' and this, apart from referring to the yearly harvest-ing of food, also relates to the wyrd, and the ultimate conse-quences of human action. People say, 'what goes around comes around', which is true, but not always in the manner, or at the time, that one expects.

In readings the Jera rune often indicates a turning point for the better, like the return of spring after a dark and cold winter. As such, it is more positive than the three preceding runes in this aett. In the runic calendar, the Jera rune is situated at Yule, the festival of the return of the sun. That time of year, or perhaps the more conventionally accepted date of 31 December, is the optimum time to do a yearly forecast with the runes. I will give an example of such a reading in the chapter on runic divination.

JERA

spiritual aspect: growth and progress
emotional or psychological aspect: patience and healing
negative aspect: harking back to the past, repeating negative patterns

EIHWAZ

This rune teaches us the mysteries of life, death and that which is in between. It is the rune of endurance and initiation as is borne out in the mythology of Odin's ordeal on Yggdrasil when he hung suspended between life and death for nine days, transcended the barriers and obtained knowledge of the runes — that is, the mysteries and laws underpinning the workings of the universe and evolution. If Jera represents time and the turning and returning of motion, Eihwaz is the pivotal point on which everything turns: the Cosmic axis, Yggdrasil itself, giving access to all the other worlds, or the physical axis on which the planet earth revolves. Here, all the forces are in balance at a point of stability, like the eye of a hurricane. A beneficial exercise is to visualize Jera spinning around Eihwaz, preferably against a backdrop of a starry night. Eihwaz is the point of equilibrium of life and death. Eihwaz is suspended between both, outside the circles of time. As Jera represents time, Eihwaz take us beyond time.

The three runes Jera, Eihwaz and the next one Perthro collectively embody the mysteries of Cosmic might. Working with these three runes together can give access to all knowledge which may be known by us humans in our present state of evolution. The Eihwaz rune is also the shamanic tree on which one can travel to other realities and obtain altered states of consciousness, in combination with the Hagalaz rune. Finally, a wand constructed in the form an Eihwaz rune, or engraved with Eihwaz runes, can serve as a powerful protective device; a portable, magical focal point of tranquillity, calm and yet immense dynamic potential.

spiritual aspect: the possibility to obtain at least temporarily cosmic consciousness

emotional or psychological aspect: inner power of stability in spite of external circumstances, endurance

negative aspect: Confusion, lack of attention, hysteria

PERTHRO

Perthro is the most mysterious rune of all. As I said before, not much is known about its meaning, and our best guesses are very speculative. The word itself has not been decisively identified as occurring elsewhere in any of the Germanic languages. My interpretation, therefore, is based largely on meditation and intuition.

When I said that I associate Perthro with birth I meant that I think this is the most extensive meaning: the birth of the universe, the externalization of consciousness, the realization and actualization of the hidden potential from the Ginnugagap, the Nordic version of the unborn universe. All knowledge is contained within Perthro, hidden in various layers of Órlog and Wyrd. It is here that wyrd is shaped, it is here records are kept. Órlog (literally, 'deep law') dictates large-scale 'destiny' or fate, the consequences of the primal laws of the universe itself. Wyrd is more individual and can be manipulated through the use of magic. For example, the occurrence of Ragnarok (the 'destiny of the Gods' or the 'twilight of the Gods', meaning a Germanic apocalypse) is dictated by Órlog; it's going to happen, whether it be by the human race blowing itself up or by the sun turning supernova at some time in the future, or an asteroid hitting the earth; whatever has a beginning has also an end, at least on one level of existence. Órlog is laid down, and cannot be altered. Personal wyrd is the tapestry of apparent cause and effect within an individual's life, which intertwines with other people's wyrd, from family and friends to the larger community; all wyrd is interwoven and interdependent. Insight into the workings of wyrd can be obtained through divination with runes and/or any other method. With the knowledge thus obtained, wyrd can be manipulated to a certain extent, depending on the magical might or hamingja available to the individual and the degree of consciousness of the individual. The Perthro rune is the doorway to the knowledge of wyrd and for this reason is mostly associated with the Norns.

PERTHRO

spiritual aspect: Well of knowledge for growth
emotional or psychological aspect: access to the individual as well as to the collective unconscious
negative aspect: delusions, fantasies, megalomania

ALGIZ

This is the rune of hallowing, warding, and access to higher spiritual awareness. As we have seen, the Algiz rune is often used in a stance to invoke the Gods. In a way it is the holiest of the runes, used to create sacred space and draw down the power of the Upper Worlds of the gods: Asgard, the realm of the Aesir; Vanaheim, the realm of the Vanir; and Alfheim, the realm of the Light elves. The latter are akin to Devic beings of Hindu tradition, and also may include the hallowed dead. Naturally, therefore, if you turn the rune upside down it can be used to access the Underworld, Hella's realm for example, the place of the mundane dead.

The Algiz rune symbolizes Bifrost, the Rainbow bridge between Midgard and Asgard. The three elements fire, water, and air comprise the rainbow, over which one travels to meet with the gods. The god Heimdallr is the guardian of the rainbow bridge, and anyone wishing to cross must gain his permission. As in other occult traditions, this may involve a test of worthiness. Algiz furthermore is strongly connected with the Valkyries, the female emanations of Odin, mythologically portrayed as his daughters. Valkyries are mostly known for their function to choose the dead and carry them off to Valhalla, but they are also involved in shielding, warding and protecting; hence their alternative name of 'shield-maidens'.

ALGIZ

spiritual aspect: invokes the highest protection
emotional or psychological aspect: communication with other realms and other parts of the self
negative aspect: none found so far

SOWULO

The last rune in the second aett represents the Sun, the solar force of life, invigoration, dedication, optimism and healing. This is another rune of power, the power of the magical will, the power to win, the confidence in oneself undeterred by other's opinions. This rune can empower the individual and confers the ability to persist in any endeavour. The Sowulo rune represents the Higher Self, the guiding light of the principles one holds. Sowulo will always inspire one to do 'the right thing'. If one is in a quandary about a difficult ethical question, meditating and invoking the Sowulo rune will often be of great help. As such Sowulo brings out the highest values and potential of the individual working with it. In adverse circumstances, focus on the Sowulo rune, as it is the rune of invincibility and final triumph.

The sun was valued greatly by our forebears. In Northern mythology the deity associated with the Sun is the goddess

Sunna, who is the conductor or chariot-driver of the Sun's life-force. Chariots on which Sun-disks have been mounted have been found in Scandinavia and mostly date from the Bronze Age. The combination of chariot and Sun-disk hints at a complementary relationship between the runes Raido and Sowulo. Raido is the principle of control, or the act of controlling whereas Sowulo can be the higher spiritual force which is in control, and/or the final goal. Thus, Sowulo can reveal the true purpose in life.

SOWULO

spiritual aspect: enlightenment
emotional or psychological aspect: confidence, optimism
negative aspect: impulsiveness, burn out

THIRD AETT

I see this as the aett of transformation. The first aett was largely concerned with the gods; the second, with the Norns, Wyrd, time and other cosmic absolutes. The third aett is concerned more with the human condition, social aspects and spiritual transformation.

TEIWAZ

Teiwaz is mostly known as a 'victory rune', especially in battle. Most of us will not be confronted with actual battle in the military sense; however, we all experience small battles throughout life, usually with other people. For most of us a shortcut to victory is a most welcome concept, but it is not that easy. This rune is ruled by Tyr, the god of justice! Not, that is, the 'justice' we associate with some cynical lawyers, authoritarian judges and corrupt politicians, but the common justice of the people. Tyr was never exclusively a war god or battle god; he is strongly involved with arbitration and the 'Thing', a folk assembly where disputes were resolved by agreements and peace was kept. Tyr, however, is uncompromising in his judgment. He is impeccably fair and even-handed. As a warrior, Tyr is motivated by a sense of justice. He may therefore be seen as a god of law and order, in a positive sense, governing social values, legal contracts and oaths.

The Teiwaz or Tyr rune can only be used to win a dispute if one is morally and ethically in the right. The power of this rune cannot be perverted for one's own ends; I have observed attempts to do so leading to disastrous consequences in some peoples' lives. This is the rune of the 'spiritual warrior' whose values are closest to what Carlos Castaneda's Don Juan describes as 'impeccability'. The shape of the rune is an arrow or a spear and as such it is a weapon which can be used to smite opposition. Less aggressively, Teiwaz, combined with Wunjo, can be called upon to resolve disputes in an even-handed manner to the benefit of the community rather than just one individual.

TEIWAZ

spiritual aspect: valour, altruism
emotional and psychological aspect: strength and honour
negative aspect: defeat

BERKANA

This, the most goddess-orientated of all runes, is mostly connected with the Vanir deities, and also with Frigga. It is the rune of motherhood, nurturing and protection, especially for children and infants. Berkana is a life-giving rune, in contrast with Teiwaz the previous rune which, as we have seen, has a death-dealing aspect. It is thus associated with the Goddess

Idun, who tends the golden apples which sustain the lives of gods and stave off old age and death. Even the gods need to be nurtured; they are not absolutely immortal, and their survival is forever dependent upon the continued, restoring energy of life itself — the fruit of mother Earth.

Berkana is one of the birth-runes which helps bring things forth, and this applies to everything from actual birthing to magical workings. This rune is magically useful for hiding and concealing things until the right time for fruition. Berkana is the rune of growth and rites of passage from one stage of life to the next, and for post-menopausal women this is a most powerful rune to work with. Berkana's creative energies of growth and bringing forth can be used for magical workings or any other creative projects.

As the rune of life, Berkana has, nevertheless, relevance to death, initiation and rebirth — for one cannot exist without the other. Similarly Teiwaz has a life aspect to it, as one man's death is another man's victory. The two runes compliment each other as Sky father and Earth mother. Both Teiwaz and Berkana represent aspects of the Tree of Life, Teiwaz as the Irminsul and Berkana as its female counterpart, the Birch.

For children, and for young girls in particular, the Berkana rune is a lovely, protective symbol. I often advise parents to obtain a silver name-plate or bracelet inscribed with their daughter's name on the outside and with three Berkana runes on the inside. This amulet, which invokes the protection of the Goddess in all her aspects, has produced favourable results.

BERKANA

spiritual aspect: growth, nurturing
emotional and psychological aspect: mature wisdom
negative aspect: immaturity, clinging, addictions

Ehwaz is, as we have seen, the rune of the horse. In human terms I relate this rune to relationships, partnerships and friendships. Horses are highly intelligent and sensitive animals; they have their likes and dislikes much like people. This I know through personal observation, having kept horses on my land on behalf of their owner. They are capable of forming a deep friendship with other horses, a friendship going further than mating matters. When the owner removed one horse, its 'friend' became very disturbed and upset, clearly missing its companion.

In any relationship, horsey or human, there is always the question of control: who is the boss. We can learn a great deal from horses; they argue and fight but they also will help each other out and co-operate. Partnerships are based on co-operation. This, of course, is also true in a committed relationship such as marriage, and this is also part of the Ehwaz package of meanings. A negatively influenced Ehwaz rune often means false friends and betrayal. The Ehwaz rune also has some bearing on the practice of divination. Tacitus recorded some divinatory practices of the Germanic tribes involving horses; for example, the behaviour of a horse was held to predict the outcome of a battle.

Horses have always been thought of as highly sacred among the Germanic peoples. Psychologically, the Ehwaz rune can teach us the art of adjusting. Whereas Raido, a rune strongly in sympathy with Ehwaz, enables us to take control of a situation, Ehwaz enables us to adjust to a situation and make the best of it. Ehwaz therefore teaches one to be flexible, adaptable and pragmatic, and to appreciate the importance of following one's instinct or gut feelings. This is not a rune associated with intellectual analysis of a situation — but as you might expect by now, given the way the runes fit together so logically, the next one clearly is!

EHWAZ

spiritual aspects: cooperation with Higher Powers
emotional and psychological aspect: instinct, intuition
negative aspect: indecisiveness, treachery

MANNAZ

This is the rune of man, the human condition, social struc-
tures and responsibilities. Like Wunjo, this rune refers to
people as a collective, be it a family, a village or a magical
fraternity; not the individual per se. Mannaz is the rune of the
rational mind as opposed to the previous rune which is more
in tune with the instinctual side. Intelligence is the greatest
power of humans, being composed of thinking and remem-
bering, the functions of Huginn and Muninn, Odin's ravens.
Mannaz is known as the rune of the perfected intellect, meld-
ing reason and intuition, with reason being the senior partner.
There is a connection with Mimir, the giant Odin consulted
with at the Well named after him: the Well of Mimir, or the
well of memories. In divination, this rune refers to people
in general. The sort of people referred to and their relationship with the querent can be deduced from the other runes
appearing with it in a reading. Inverted Mannaz sometimes
indicates an enemy, although alternatively, I have seen it
(non-pejoratively) denoting a male homosexual. In readings
Mannaz may suggest legal affairs and matters of mutual
cooperation, especially when it occurs in conjunction with
Ehwaz. Together with Raido, it will often denote assistance
from, or counsel given by people.

Magically, this rune can be used to attract support from one's
peer group in a dispute. Combined in a bind-rune with Ansuz, it
can be employed to win an intellectual argument or pass an
examination. Both runes strengthen the mind when necessity

arises. An even stronger sigil for this purpose can be constructed by adding Raido and Ehwaz to the bind-rune.

MANNAZ

spiritual aspect: intelligent awareness, open-mindedness
emotional and psychological aspect: awareness of kinship with all humans as part of the greater whole
negative aspect: intellectual arrogance, bigotry

LAGUZ

The meaning of the Laguz rune, as we have seen, is at first glance, water, sea or lake. This is the rune of 'the deep', the hidden ebb and flow of the currents of life. Laguz is a very occult rune, associated with deep undercurrents of the collective unconscious, seeping up into reality and shaping wyrd. A visit to Loch Ness, for example (with or without seeing the monster!) can convey an appreciation of the meaning of the Laguz Rune.

Laguz has a sympathetic resonance with Perthro, as both are interconnected in the Well of Wyrd, metaphorically and psychologically. In dreams, water is often representative of the emotions. As the emotions often precede and give direction to action, they are, first and foremost, the medium of shaping wyrd. If we can understand and master, rather than suppress, emotions, it is possible to manipulate wyrd. By diving into the deep of one's own mind, accessing all negative or hindering emotional baggage, without fear or favour, and using the knowledge thus obtained constructively to 're-write the script', so to speak, the individual can evolve and grow, turning problems into helpful lessons for personal and spiritual growth.

The Laguz rune, being representative of water, can also be perceived as symbolizing the 'etheric' or 'astral' forces. Water will assume the shape of any container it is poured into; so too

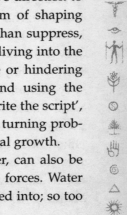

will astral substance take the shape of whatever the imaginative will of the magician dictates. The Laguz rune therefore can be used for all magical workings involving astral plane work.

LAGUZ

spiritual aspect: empathy, sympathy

emotional and psychological aspect: the deep mind and the collective unconscious

negative aspect: manipulative wingeing, emotional black-mail, lack of moral fibre

INGUZ

The Inguz rune is closely connected to the earth and the land, as is the next rune, Othala. Inguz especially is the rune for 'seed', gestation and germination. Frey, as we have seen, is the god of vegetation and food, and he is in that respect the Lord of the good earth, the nourishing earth. Yes, the earth is female and often seen correctly as the mother of all that live on her, but she cannot create alone. The Inguz rune then represents the male, fertilizing aspect of nature. But that's only one half of the story; the shape of the Inguz rune is also reminiscent of the female genitalia. This rune then contains elements of both genders; perhaps this is the reason that in modern Asatru the god Frey is very often the patron god of homosexual men, and 'straight' men who have integrated their female side.

To complicate matters even more, Inguz is also associated with children, both female and male. As Berkana is the rune of pregnancy and Perthro the rune of birth, Inguz is the rune of the child. In Anglo-Saxon and Frisian, patronymic names were formed by adding -ing after the father's forename; this is the usual significance of the '-ing' in names like Bunting and Hadding which are found in England and Holland. The old

Swedish royal family was called the Ynglingar; they were supposedly descended from Yngvi Frey. As discussed earlier the
Anglo-Saxon form of Inguz duplicated gives a shape resem-
bling the DNA double helix.

Like Gebo, Inguz is perfectly symmetrical in shape, and looks
the same from all angles; and when we combine these two symmetrical runes into a single figure, we get the next rune in the
futhark: Othala.

INGUZ

spiritual aspect: complete integration of the four Selves:
physical, emotional, mental and spiritual
emotional and psychological aspect: the inner child
negative aspect: frivolity, immaturity

OTHALA

This, the penultimate rune in the futhark, is the rune associated
with inheritance. When we look at this in connection with the
previous rune Inguz, see that the shape of Othala is a combination of Inguz and Gebo, and Othala can thus be interpreted as
the 'gift of Ing'. Esoterically, then, the concept of inheritance can
be seen as the genetic material that is passed on from parent to
child. This material, physically speaking, has all the genetic
components, either active or dormant, of the whole of the
human race (and possibly more than that).

Having mentioned the word 'race', it must be said that this is
one of the runes which has been defiled in the past, to justify
racism. The rune Othala does indeed represent the inheritance
of ancestral lands by particular descendants, a concept which is
easily abused. In its broadest meaning, of course, the Othala
rune refers to the inheritance by the whole of humanity of the
planet itself and the inherent responsibilities thereof. It is no

longer a matter of natives inheriting their lands, be they German, Celtic or native Americans; we all, collectively, have inherited the planet itself, and this, the most precious heritage, is all we have to pass on to our descendants.

Spiritually, the Othala rune can be used to invoke Odin in his aspect of wanderer and teacher. Odin, as we have seen with Ansuz and Wunjo, has three main aspects ascribed to him: mythologically the other two are his brothers. The three brothers are Odin, Vili and Ve; names which correspond to his aspects of warrior, shaman and wanderer, respectively. Besides being one of Odin's names, 'Ve' also means 'sacred enclosure', which was that part of the hof or temple where only the officiating gothar or priests had access. It was the place where the ritual regalia was kept. The Othala rune has been associated with an enclave by other rune-workers, and an enclave invokes images of safety and protection. It is mythologically comparable to the walls of Asgard, which were built as a protection against the giants.

OTHALA

spiritual aspect: connectedness with all Earthdwellers
emotional and psychological aspect: love for one's home and security thereof
negative aspect: racism, xenophobia, greed

DAGAZ

This is, in my opinion, the correct last rune in the futhark. Some ancient rune-rows show Dagaz in this position, whereas others show Othala, with Dagaz as the penultimate rune. So, both interpretations are possible, historically. Scholarly convention favours Othala, but the reasons why I prefer to see Dagaz last are metaphysical in nature. When the runes are laid out in a circle, the last rune appears opposite Jera, and as Jera represents the winter solstice when the darkness is greatest, Dagaz represents the summer solstice when the light is strongest. Thus, like Jera, Dagaz is a rune of change. Jera, as mentioned previously, is the rune of gentle change, whereas Dagaz is the rune of cataclysmic change. Whenever energy reaches a saturation point, it is forcefully converted into its opposite nature. Whatever is fully positive will turn into a negative. At this point, Dagaz fuses with Fehu and initiates a new cycle.

Dagaz is a rune with many layers of kenning. It represents the end of an era and the beginning of the next cycle. It acts as a catalyst, initiating change without changing its own nature. Dagaz is the rune of transcendence. Most of the runes partake of Fire and Ice, some are Fire and some are Ice, some are both or neither; Dagaz is one of the runes which transcends this duality. Dagaz goes beyond duality to synthesis, unity and the emergence of another reality. Dagaz is the rune which can confer cosmic consciousness or enlightenment. Dagaz can be used to combine other runes in a synergistic bind-rune. Braiding and weaving runes chosen for a specific working into the framework of Dagaz will fuse their energies and combine their powers to be used for an act of magical intent.

On a very mundane level, Dagaz can be used to hide things from view. An experiment with this could be conducted as follows: select an object such as a photograph of someone or a vase, place this in a fairly prominent position in a room (but not too obvious), trace a Dagaz rune over the object, with the intent of making it invisible, and see whether anyone notices it. Likewise, with practice one can shield oneself in Dagaz and become invisible to other people; what happens is that they don't consciously register you. It is extremely helpful in jumping queues and this has, on several occasions, saved me a great deal of time and bother!

DAGAZ

spiritual aspect: total enlightenment
emotional and psychological aspect: positive focus in life
negative aspect: destructive impulsiveness

DIVINATION WITH RUNES

Divination is an art, in which some practitioners are more naturally gifted than others; but most people, nevertheless, have sufficient innate ability to become reasonably proficient — be it with tarot, astrology or the runes. The runes differ from more familiar, widespread divinatory systems in that they are, on face value, only twenty-four angular signs. They are more sparse in appearance than tarot decks for example, which might seem a disadvantage. However, as we shall see, these simple forms have a remarkable capacity to stimulate the clairvoyant imagination.

Competent rune-workers disdain the use of the so-called 'blank rune' — a spurious modern innovation, without any traditional meaning. After all, there are no such things as blank letters of the alphabet or blank tarot cards! This bogus practice probably started when some foolish novice bought a set of runes from a supplier whose habit was to make one or two blank slips of wood as *spares* with each rune-set, so that if a rune were lost or damaged, it could easily be replaced just by carving it on the blank. The ignorant buyer must have assumed the blank pieces had some significance of their own — eventually incorporating this idea into badly-researched literature on the runes. Whatever the case may be, there is no doubt that the twenty-four-rune system of the Elder futhark is complete in itself and needs no modern, New Age additions. The numerology works well: there are twenty-four hours in a day, twelve months in a year and eight recognized festivals in modern Pagan tradition, Nordic as well as Celtic. The blank rune muddles up and invalidates this rich system of correspondences.

To be able to divine with runes one has to develop a high degree of intuition and invest a measure of trust in one's own ability. To be able to perceive accurate data relevant to someone having a reading, one must make a sympathetic link with the runes and even more important, one must imprint the subconscious mind with each one of them. This has to be done on at least two levels. Firstly, one must read everything one can about runes, but with a critical mind, asking questions all the way, and referring always to one's own understanding. (A reading list will be provided at the end of this book.) Second, to infuse the runic symbols into the deep mind, use them for art! Play with them to make pictures; write your name in runes and see whether the runes of your name spell out something you recognize as part of your personality; combine the rune of your name into an aesthetically pleasing sigil and use this as a signature to mark your personal property, such as books. For those who are right-handed, draw runes with the left and visa versa; this will link in with the intuitive part of the brain in the right hemisphere. Simple exercises like these, enjoyable in themselves, will give intuitive understanding of the meaning of runes. A daily meditation on one rune in futhark order, with notes taken of any thought coming up during the meditation, will prove most helpful; it will lay the basis in twenty-four days for a practical working knowledge of the runes. After this, do the same exercise again but at random. Just pull a rune out of the pouch and observe over the next twenty-four hours any events that take place, no matter how apparently insignificant, which are in keeping with the meaning of the rune. A silly but accurate example would be if the rune is Raido inverted, and the next day you miss the bus! Observe and record simple happenings like this, for future reference. If you are sceptically minded, it might occur to you that something is bound to happen, each day, that would fit *any* of the runes, so the connections you observe are just 'coincidence'. This is partly true, but it misses the point. By routinely observing 'coincidences', you stimulate your clairvoyant instincts — to the point where, increasingly, you just *know* that something specific is going to happen as soon as you look at the rune. And when it *does* happen, just as you expect, you will know this is beyond coincidence.

When you feel ready, ask a simple question, pull one or more runes and see whether their meaning can be interpreted as an answer. On your birthday, draw a circle with twelve segments. Pull one rune in each one, note them down and see whether they forecast something over the next twelve months. After a year you will recognize when looking back that certain runes did mean certain things. You can also do all of these little exercises for your friends and family — just to get familiarity with the runes, their meanings and how to interpret them, in the light of specific issues. Runes are excellent for answering questions; they give a direct, accurate answer if the question is properly phrased, including simple yes/no questions.

You should, at some point, make your own set of runes, preferably from the wood of a fruitbearing tree. Avoid commercially-produced runes, which are sometimes supplied with books. If you have difficulty crafting your own runes, ask a trusted friend or kinsman/woman to make them for you, in exchange for an appropriate gift. Runes are magical tools; therefore it is wise to consider whose energy they will carry as well as your own. Once you have made your runes, you have to infuse them with personal might. Make them your own; sleep with them in a pouch carried under your clothing, around your neck or waist. After nine days and nights, construct a simple dedication ceremony in which you ask for the blessing of the gods or goddesses of your choice. Especially recommended are Odin, Freyja and the Norns. However, having asked for the help and blessing of the god/desses in this way, if you should ever make money out of a reading it is strongly recommended that you give nine per cent of your earnings to a charity, preferably an environmental one; trees or animals for instance.

Runic divination is a kind of mediumship, in which one has to mediate between the querent and the runes and interpret messages from spiritual levels, of which the physical rune-stones or rune-staves are focal points or doorways. Divination is, in origin, a sacred act of asking counsel from the gods, as the word 'divine', from which divination is derived, clearly suggests. Long-term forecasts, however, cannot be as detailed. They may contain contradictions as well, since before they are realized the individual concerned may make certain decisions or carry out various actions, which will have changed the pattern of the web. There is no such thing as a fixed future; there is only the web, which appears to us in time-bound and space-bound conditions as past, present and future. In reality, the web is a complex whole and, when understood as such, can be utilized to exercise a degree of control over one's circumstances. The so-called 'past' is actually part of the present; it is that part of one's wyrd which actively creates and shapes current circumstances. As such, the past is not a clear-cut, separate realm of non-existence; it has not ceased its influence on the so-called present. By means of divination, it is possible to gain information concerning a specific aspect of the web, for example the past. Because the web is an integral whole, any interference with one part of the web causes reverberations in other parts of it.

Once the information needed has been acquired, magic can be applied. Magic is the act of interfering in one part of the web through operation of the will and thereby deliberately altering wyrd. The power of magic and divination in the Northern Tradition is most strongly associated with Odin. These powers in terms of past, present and hypothetical future time are identified with the three goddesses or Norns: Urd, Verdandi and Skuld, who weave the web of fate or orlog. Divination has a close relationship with magic. After all, there is little point in investigating future probabilities if not with the intent to magically manipulate these probabilities in one's favour. Definite predictions can certainly occur as part of a rune reading, but usually happen spontaneously and not necessarily under the conscious control of the reader. If you view divination solely as a means of prediction, you will find that it is not reliable. This is only to be expected, since matters which are hidden in the future and predestined are usually unavoidable and form part of a person's own wyrd — they are consequences of one's own past actions, one's own being and inner nature. But the more the individual is conscious of the hidden side of Nature and of his own self, the more control he has over his circumstances, in which case it is all the less likely that undesirable 'predictions' will come true.

PROFESSIONAL ETHICS

Two simple ethical principles should be followed when doing readings for other people, commercially or otherwise. Firstly, no matter how bad the reading looks, *never predict a disaster*, merely point out dangers and suggest ways of minimizing them. Second, *don't assume expertise you don't possess*; instead, give accurate advice on who to turn to for specific needs. For example, I've picked up more than once on serious medical conditions in a client; in cases like this, never speculate — just tell them in the strongest possible terms to have a check up as soon as possible. When doing readings on a regular basis in your own area, familiarize yourself with support agencies such as: local Citizen's Advice Bureaus, social services, rape crisis centres, STD and family planning clinics, Samaritans, etc, so that when you encounter a particular problem, you can offer the client a sympathetic hearing but refer them on!

Third, *respect your client's confidentiality*. To be a decent psychic consultant, one has to develop a working ethic similar to a priest(ess) or social worker. If you decide to 'go professional' in this field, it will be very helpful to take a course in co-counselling. Most local authorities run affordable courses in this field. Many people coming for readings are lonely and troubled, perhaps going through one of the familiar life-crises: adolescence, parenthood, menopause, or retirement. Rather than dazzling displays of your psychic powers, such people really want a sympathetic ear and some common sense advice. Sometimes, however, one may come across a serious problem case, such as people with evident psychiatric needs. A young lad once came up to me in Camden Psychic centre insisting he was 'The Beast', and looking for confirmation by begging every psychic there to find the number 666 tattooed on his body! If you take up reading professionally, you will meet someone like this before too long! However, most people are relatively normal — and common sense, a sense of humour and objectivity will go long way.

EXERCISES FOR BEGINNERS

If you are a complete newcomer to psychic readings, I can suggest a way to gain some practice and experience, firstly in developing the ability to 'see' and deduce certain facts from the layout of the runes, and secondly, in presenting the information to the client. You may be highly intuitive in picking up things but not very skilled in communicating them in a manner that is helpful and comprehensible. Buy a daily newspaper or a woman's magazine and turn to the problem page. Pick a problem letter and, *without* reading the agony aunt's comments first, do a reading on it, as if the letter-writer were your client. Copy the letter out and lay it in the middle of your cloth, focus on it and lay the runes out face down, turn the runes over and see whether the runes correspond at all with the issues written about. Then imagine you have to speak to a client and advise her or him: how would you put the information into words; how would you present it? Only then, read what the agony aunt has said. It will be mundane, of course, but usually reasonable, common-sense advice — and professional agony aunts (or uncles) have to be able to write clearly and comprehensibly.

To develop some real clairvoyance, get a friend to select a problem-letter from a paper or magazine and write it out; have her seal this in an envelope and lay it in front of you as you do a reading. Try to see whether the runes make sense. At first, look at the runes and try to 'guess' what the possible issues are in the letter, and write your impressions down. Then open the envelope and compare your impressions with the actual letter. Give yourself marks out of ten. Do this once a week and keep a diary or journal of the results. You will soon find that you're getting accurate readings.

CONSULTING THE RUNES

Runes can be consulted by two main methods: casting and laying of the runes. The most ancient method is described by the Roman historian Tacitus in chapter 10 of his *Germania* (c 98 CE). A branch was cut from a nut-bearing tree and cut into slips, on which 'signs' were written; these slips then were thrown randomly onto a white cloth. After this the priest, or if the reading was private, the head of the household would utter a silent prayer to the gods; facing northwards, he would take three slips, one after the other, and interpret their meanings. The signs used in Tacitus' time have not survived, but they were almost certainly early versions of the runes. Similar casting techniques are mentioned in Icelandic sagas, written down some twelve centuries later; the technique, therefore, stood the test of time! Casting the runes, then, is basically the technique of throwing them from a cup or a pouch onto a white cloth, on which may be embroidered a design outlining specific areas with special meanings — for example, a circle divided into twelve or eight segments.

The advantage of casting the runes is that it allows the powers that be — or the forces of chaos, if you prefer — to determine the cast, which can then be interpreted as a whole.

Alternatively, one may prefer, as I do, a more controlled method whereby the runes are laid face down and selected by the querent. This can be done by moving the hand slowly and deliberately over the runes, asking oneself if they feel hot or cold. Selecting them on this basis, one at a time, the querent lays the runes out on the cloth, face down, according to a predetermined pattern (I will discuss various layouts later on). The reader then turns up the runes one after another and interprets each one in the light of its position. When using a structured layout, the interpretation can be enhanced by cross-referring each rune with those in related positions (such as the opposite side of a square, for instance). This can suggest deeper insights and subtleties which contribute to a thorough consultation. The advantage of this method is that the subconscious of the querent can guide the hand while selecting relevant runes, and thus will communicate specific issues to be discussed.

Before we look at practical examples of reading the runes one final aspect of the theory of runic divination must be discussed: the distinction between invertible and non-invertible runes. An invertible rune is a rune which, when placed upside-down, looks different from its positive or upright version. Thus, for example, Fehu: ᚠ is normally shown in its upright form, but inverted it looks like:. ᚠ Fehu is therefore an invertible rune. However, Eihwaz, when placed upside-down, looks the same:ᛇ. It is therefore a noninvertible rune. Only fifteen out of the twenty-four runes can be inverted, while nine runes of special power cannot. Inversion of runes negates the meaning of those runes in their positive upright positions and consequently turns their meanings upside down. A very simple example would be Fehu. At its most basic level, it would normally mean money. Inverted Fehu, however, would mean lack of money. Clearly, this reversal of meaning is only possible when the runes actually can be turned upside-down.

Sometimes it can be difficult to know whether the light-meaning or the dark-meaning side of the rune is shown in any given reading. For example, Uruz inverted may be interpreted as a weakness. Uruz inverted therefore takes on the meaning of the opposite of Uruz upright. Thurisaz, however, as we have seen, is quite aggressive in its normal upright mode; inverted it becomes more defensive rather than aggressive and may therefore take on a more positive function. Different spreads may be used to define what is helpful and what is an obstacle; it may also be good to phrase your question so as to leave no doubt, for instance: 'What kind of problems will I face in my new job?' In a more general reading, certain runes, which I refer to below as 'companion runes', may help to brighten the aspects of others: if the rune in the primary place is companioned well, its better meanings may be taken, but if it is companioned with one or more of the darker or more difficult runes, it may represent

an upcoming challenge. Some of the runic meanings or divinatory indications overlap; when these runes appear together, it strengthens whatever aspects they have in common.

BASIC GUIDELINES IN RUNIC MEANINGS FOR DIVINATION

The basic meanings of the runes applied in divination are listed below. These are only generalizations and guidelines. Do not apply them mechanically — always use your own intuition and judgement first. These meanings are very simple and on the most basic level serve as the background for a straightforward reading, in which questions of a practical nature can be answered.

Fehu: Financial strength and prosperity of the client in the present and near future; inverted or in combination with Nauthiz, Isa or Hagalaz: possible indebtedness.

In questions of finance: money or trouble with money, quarrels over money
In questions of romance: sexual attraction or jealousy
In questions of health: life-force or fever
In questions of the workplace: energy, financial improvement or trouble with co-workers, burnout

Companion runes: Gebo, Jera, Berkana, Inguz

Uruz: Health matters, positive or otherwise depending on other runes selected; with Thurisaz or Teiwaz, possible surgery. Inverted usually a lack of physical stamina. Natural aspect: rain, water. Vital strength, cleansing, healing. Badly aspected, it can show uncontrolled power.

In questions of finance: vigour or an uncontrolled investment
In questions of romance: welcome strength and energy or coming on too strongly
In questions of health: good health, healing; always a good rune
In questions of the workplace: enthusiasm or a bull in a china shop approach

Companion runes: Perthro, Algiz, Laguz

Thurisaz: Conflicts and complexities of an aggressive nature, disputes, psychological problems. Thurisaz, Thorn. Natural aspect: thunderstorms. 'Thurse', an elemental giant. Lightning, breakthrough, disruption, aggressive male sexuality, battering down barriers. The 'thorn' can also be the thorn of awakening. Used in warding and in works related to magical and/or bodily combat.

In questions of finance: disruption, conflict
In questions of romance: strong male energy or badly disruptive male energy
In questions of health: for a male, the genitals; for a female, harm or pain to the feminine parts
In questions of the workplace: a strong attack, trouble, strife

Companion runes: Uruz, Algiz, Sowulo

Ansuz: Communications and transmissions; points things back to sources in the past. Also authority, elders, possible promotions in job-related readings. Natural aspect: wind. 'God': Odin.

In questions of finance: answers, open paths of communication, advice or bad advice

In questions of romance: communication
In questions of health: relates to the lungs, air-passages, mouth and throat
In questions of the workplace: communication, inspiration

Companion runes: Raido, Kenaz, Wunjo, Mannaz

Raido: What is right or not right; what move to make; decision making. Travelling, journeys, moving house or job. Natural aspect: the sun's journey. 'Riding'. Timing, ritual activity, especially dance and processions, proportion, legal matters. A journey; used magically to ensure that a journey goes well and safely.

In questions of finance: regularity, consistency
In questions of romance: the relationship is proceeding on the proper path
In questions of health: a gradual, natural process of healing or a slow decline
In questions of the workplace: regular progression; may also show an upcoming business trip or change of job

Companion runes: Jera, Algiz, Sowulo, Ehwaz

Kenaz: Opening up of new ways, opportunities, information, solutions, creativity, studies. Natural aspect: burning, decay. 'Torch', also 'boil or sore'. Craftsmanship, dissolution and recreation; the raw power of Fehu controlled. Its darker side is dissolution without reformulation.

In questions of finance: control
In questions of romance: sexual energies sublimated or directed towards a goal
In questions of health: infection, inflammation

Companion runes: Uruz, Teiwaz, Inguz

Gebo: All matters of an exchanging nature: contracts, personal relationships. Gifts, favours and obligations. Agreements of a reciprocal nature. Exchange of power or money, a wedding, a relationship between equals, a two-way flow of communication, mutual oath-taking, mutual loyalty. Also the relationships of sacrifice and blessing between humans and the god/desses.

In questions of finance: a good partnership
In questions of romance: a good relationship
In questions of health: balance, taking care of one's body properly
In questions of the workplace: a good working partnership

Companion runes: Ehwaz, Mannaz, Othala

Wunjo: Gain, accomplishments, that which is wished for. Success. When inverted or badly aspected with other runes: caution. Natural aspect: warmth. 'Joy'. Happiness, calm, the well-integrated ego, friendship and clan- or oath-fellowship; badly aspected: blindness to danger or trouble.

In questions of finance: security or a false sense of security
In questions of romance: contentment or blindness to deception
In questions of health: good health, the immune system
In questions of the workplace: a sense of satisfaction

Companion runes: Uruz, Gebo, Algiz, Sowulo, Othala

Hagalaz: The uncontrolled forces in the unconscious originating from the past, of a disruptive nature causing changes for the long-term good. Short-term disappointments and possible loss. Natural aspect: hail. In divination, this rune most often shows a major disruption which, if one stands firm, can resolve into a better situation.

In questions of finance: a sudden disruptive shock
In questions of romance: a new person or event intruding
In questions of health: a sudden difficulty or attack
In questions of the workplace: surprise, disruption, a major change

Companion runes: Uruz, Raido, Eihwaz, Sowulo

Nauthiz: Restrictive forces, fears, anxieties, feelings of guilt, sometimes poverty. Also often a warning and therefore a possible help: forewarned is forearmed. Natural aspect: fire, 'Need'. The need-fire (fire kindled by friction), a strengthening trial, achievement won through effort, cleansing. The ability to 'write around' Wyrd.

In questions of finance: unusual care or effort needed to improve things; hard work will make you better off than before
In questions of romance: trouble ahead; effort is needed to make the relationship work, but it is worth it
In questions of health: a strain which ultimately will make you stronger
In questions of the workplace: a serious challenge

Companion runes: Kenaz, Eihwaz, Dagaz

Isa: Blocks, stultified conditions, grievances, anything that the individual is not prepared to let go of, obstacles, delays, inactivity, frustrations. Natural aspect: 'Ice'. Immobility, absence of energy, solidification, blockage or lack of change. Also stability, peace and the cohesiveness of the ego. The antithesis of Fehu in all ways.

In questions of finance: frozen cash-flow
In questions of romance: an icy reception, loss of feelings
In questions of health: low vital force, but also consolidation, an end to pain, the halting of a difficulty
In questions of the workplace: nothing happening, no gain

Companion runes: Wunjo, Othala

Jera: Hopes and expectations, turning points, gradual changes for the better, results of earlier actions, pay offs and improvements. Natural aspect: the turning of the year, the growing of plants; 'Year' or 'harvest'. Cyclic progression, natural development, rewards coming in the course of time; also used for fruitfulness and fulfilment. The turning of Wyrd.

In questions of finance: investments paying off, plans coming to maturity
In questions of romance: a relationship coming to fullness
In questions of health: regular improvement, fertility
In questions of the workplace: fulfilment, improvement

Companion runes: Fehu, Berkana, Inguz, Dagaz

Eihwaz: The driving forces and motivations, sense of purpose. Challenges and tests. Endurance, courage and daring. Natural aspect: yew-tree, 'Yew'. The World-Tree. Death, initiation,

sudden transformation. The soul surviving the body's death, the reclaiming and awakening of ancestral memories and power in oneself, inner strength. Also used in dealing with the dead (a risky practice at best). Odin's self-sacrifice on the World-Tree.

> In questions of finance: a major transformation
> In questions of romance: deep feelings expressed
> In questions of health: the skeletal system, revival of strength; also, hereditary factors coming out
> In questions of the workplace: a major crisis

Companion runes: Wunjo, Sowulo, Mannaz, Othala

Perthro: The deepest creative part of the unconscious, the hidden realm of higher material that is waiting to come to fruition and birth, hidden talents, occult or psychic abilities. Unexpected positive changes. Natural aspect: fruit, a well, a womb. 'Lot-cup'. The Well of Wyrd, divination, the workings of Wyrd becoming manifest, also birth and the first setting of wyrd which shapes all that comes after it.

> In questions of finance: an apparently random event which cannot be avoided, with good or ill effects depending on the rest of the reading
> In questions of romance: discovery of whether or not a relationship is meant to be
> In questions of health: the female parts, genetic inheritance from the mother's side
> In questions of the workplace: the fulfilment of whatever conditions currently hold

Companion runes: Kenaz, Berkana, Inguz

Algiz: Influences which will protect you, religious aspirations. Higher spiritual awareness, assistance from higher powers or in the form of spiritual guidance by a teacher or mentor. Natural aspect: elk, swan. Warding, might summoned down from the worlds above, knowledge and inspiration coming from the god/desses.

In questions of finance: security, good yield
In questions of romance: a spiritual relationship
In questions of health: good health, protection from disease and difficulties
In questions of the workplace: security, ambition

Companion runes: Gebo, Sowulo, Dagaz

Sowulo: energy, power, enthusiasm, positive thoughts, success and accomplishments. Good physical health. Natural aspect: the sun. 'Sun'. The will, success, rulership, holiness. Safe passage through difficulties. Badly aspected: insensitivity and arrogance.

In questions of finance: good fortune, perseverance
In questions of romance: things are likely to go well
In questions of health: endurance, a positive attitude
In questions of the workplace: ambition, success

Companion runes: Wunjo, Teiwaz

Teiwaz: Personal strengths, taking initiatives, honour and justice, leadership and authority. Competitiveness in business or sport. Physical activities. 'Tyr'. Victory, bravery, stability, honour; this rune was carved upon weapons. Badly aspected: legalism and oppression of the spirit by regulations.

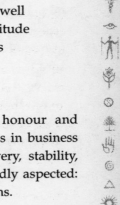

In questions of finance: legalistic matters will be of great importance, either helping or hindering according to the rest of the reading

In questions of romance: lack of flexibility, conventionality
In questions of health: strength and order; if a problem exists, standard medical treatments will be either highly recommended or should be supplemented with alternative forms of healing, depending on how the rune is aspected
In questions of the workplace: rules and regulations

Companion runes: Raido, Wunjo, Sowulo

Berkana: Fertility, birth, rebirth, growth, maternity, family life, feminine Mysteries. New beginnings and opportunities, healing and rejuvenation. Natural aspect: a birch-tree, a peat bog. 'Birch'. Birth and bringing into being, concealment, nurturing, gestation and the womb, protection, fruitfulness, secrecy. Also death, as the goddess Hel ('The Concealer').

In questions of finance: an investment which will prove to be fruitful
In questions of romance: strong female energy; if badly aspected, a smothering or unfriendly woman
In questions of health: fertility, female parts, hormonal balance
In questions of the workplace: a dominant female figure or secrets being kept

Companion runes: Kenaz, Perthro, Jera, Inguz

Ehwaz: Adaptability, joint efforts, cooperation, sexuality. Natural aspect: a horse. 'Horse'. Relationships (especially superior/inferior relationships), wedding or partnership, control; also travel, communication of holy wisdom, finding the means to make achievement possible. Odin's steed Sleipnir. Recklessness, betrayal by false friends when inverted, broken trust.

In questions of finance: a partnership, general success
In questions of romance: a solid relationship
In questions of health: how it is aspected shows the overall physical condition
In questions of the workplace: partnership; shows how you are working with superiors, inferiors, or team members

Companion runes: Raido, Gebo, Inguz

Mannaz: People at large, attitude towards others, other people's attitudes towards you, legal matters, friends and enemies, intellectual pursuits, favourable for exams when paired with Ansuz. Natural aspect: the human mind. 'Human being'. Intelligence, memory, the realizing of our godly inheritance, the conscious mind, the reaching of full mental and spiritual potential. Used for mental skills and wisdom.

In questions of finance: a decision to be made which will require much thought
In questions of romance: a close soul-mate or a purely intellectual relationship
In questions of health: indicates mental health and the brain
In questions of the workplace: intellectual effort will be required

Companion runes: Ansuz, Kenaz, Sowulo

Laguz: Emotions, stability, imagination, psychic matters, affections. Natural aspect: water (flowing water for weal, stagnant water for woe). 'Water' (also called laukaz, 'leek'). Life-force, concealment and bringing forth, cleansing, particularly against poison. The subconscious, secrets. Badly aspected: something destructive in hiding or about to come forth.

> In questions of finance: a steady flow
>
> In questions of romance: strong attraction or destructive secrets being kept
>
> In questions of health: life-force, the bloodstream; badly aspected, shows a need for cleansing
>
> In questions of the workplace: a steady stream of work, something about to be revealed

Companion runes: Uruz, Ansuz, Algiz, Sowulo

Inguz: Integration, gestation, expectations, progeny. Natural aspect: a seed. 'Ing', or Freyr. Self-sacrifice, the planting of a seed, fruitfulness. In the form ◇ , the castrated male; in the form ♦, the whole male.

> In questions of finance: good fortune, the start of a fruitful enterprise
>
> In questions of romance: a promising relationship that may call for some self-sacrifice to make it work
>
> In questions of health: the male parts, hormonal balance, sexuality in general
>
> In questions of the workplace: the start of fruitful endeavours

Companion runes: Kenaz, Gebo, Jera, Berkana

Othala: Home country, spiritual heritage, house, land properties, established fundamental values, conservative. Natural aspect: 'Udal (inherited) lands'. Family matters, ancestral possessions or powers, inheritance, the kin-soul. The border between the human world and the 'wild space' outside.

  In questions of finance: an inheritance, a solid investment, matters affecting the home
  In questions of romance: a stable, long-term relationship
  In questions of health: inherited conditions, good or bad according to how the rune is aspected
  In questions of the workplace: a stable, long-term job

Companion runes: Ansuz, Gebo, Wunjo, Eihwaz, Mannaz

Dagaz: Position between light and darkness, traversing between the worlds. Cosmic consciousness, change from one thing into its opposite, new beginnings. With negative runes possible violent destruction. Natural aspect: 'Day' (or, more properly, 'dawn'). A sudden burst of illumination, transcendent spiritual unity, fulfilment. In all matters, this rune shows fulfillment, inspiration, and the sudden beginning of better things.

EXAMPLE READINGS AND SPREADS

1. A THREE RUNE SPREAD:
URD, VERDANDI AND SKULD

This spread is mostly known to be associated with the three Norns or goddesses of fate, Urd, Verdandi and Skuld. Urd means 'that which has been', Verdandi means 'that which is becoming' and Skuld means 'that which should be'. This is interpreted as past, present and future. The simplest and often

the most effective reading is a three rune spread. There are various ways of doing this depending on what type of runes you have made. Round or square runes are best for casting, rectangular ones are more suitable for a spread.

Three Rune Spread: Uruz, Sowulo and Wunjo

The question is job related. M is in a dead-end but relatively safe job, the wages aren't terrific but there is at least some job security. However, she has been told by a friend that there is a better paid job available in New Zealand, with prospects of valuable training and the possibility of promotion. The question is therefore 'Shall I go for it?'

The Runes are: Uruz Wunjo Sowulo.

This is very clear and direct — it says: *Go for it! Big time!*

Uruz in the first place means: *This is an opportunity not to be missed; it is earned from your past actions. You deserve it.* The first place is associated with *Urd*, 'that which has been'.

Sowulo in the second place reaffirms this, as the second place is associated with *Verdandi*, or the becoming-present: it indicates success, enjoyment and lots of sunshine.

Wunjo in the third place, the place of Skuld, 'That which must be', reinforces all of the above, through its meaning of joy and perfection. Based on these runes I would say this person cannot go wrong in taking the offer, it is unlikely that such an opportunity will come along twice!

Now, this is a very simple Runic divination, but nevertheless, it may lead to a complete change of life for M.

R has a different problem. He's due to undergo minor, but necessary, surgery and is rather afraid. He is actually thinking of refusing, as he has a phobia about anaesthetics, due to an unpleasant experience as a child.

The rune-worker does not deal directly with medical problems unless of course he or she is qualified in that field and doing readings is a secondary job or hobby. The objective here, on the contrary, is to get to the bottom of R's fears, to increase his confidence so that he can face the operation calmly.

Three Rune Spread: Isa, Laguz inverted, Gebo

Isa here represents the trauma in his early childhood when, it appears, he had a tonsillectomy and felt as if he was choking. Laguz inverted tells me that he has serious unresolved emotional problems with this issue and really should receive some psychological counselling as his fears are deeply seated within the subconscious. Gebo, however, as the outcome, is clearly stating that the operation itself holds no danger at all; his problem is totally subjective and should be dealt with accordingly. It would help if R cut down on the smoking a few weeks before the anaesthetic!

2 A NINE-FOLD SPREAD: THE NINE WORLDS

For the purposes of this spread, I have correlated the nine worlds of Northern Mythology to the nine-fold division of the psycho/somatic complex as stated by Carl Gustav Jung, probably the most spiritually advanced psychiatrist of this century. This system is more complicated and requires some study of the Norse Myths as well as getting familiar with the theories of Jung. However, doing a reading in this format can deliver a wealth of useful data, on all levels of being. Indeed, a whole reading can be devoted to a particular level, for instance, the level of the soul, or the level of the personality, or spiritual levels of a higher order; thus, a very thorough consultation might involve three readings of nine runes each. All of these will overlap at some point, but the approach is generally useful.

One can narrow things down and fine tune a reading by means of follow-up readings — looking at the previous reading's information from a different perspective. For example, if a psychological reading gives certain data which suggest a need for further enquiry one can then use the same nine-fold cloth but this time from the perspective of the soul. The third type of reading is purely for those people who accept the reality of gods and goddesses, never mind in what form; so a consultation with the god or goddess directly can be obtained through the mediation of the runes and the reader, if at all sympathetic toward the idea of 'the Gods'. I will offer my opinion as to what god/dess goes with what square, but those of you who want to take things further should seek a religious commitment to these gods, before proceeding. Information about this will be offered in the appendix of this book.

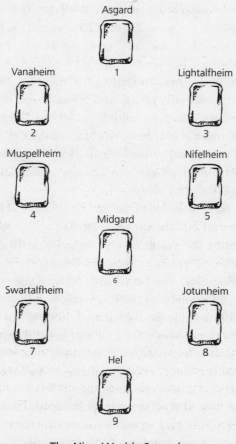

The Nine Worlds Spread

Nine Worlds: the significance of each position in the spread

1 *Asgard,* the realm of the Gods, ruled by *Odin*. In a reading, any rune placed here denotes higher spiritual ambitions, Higher Self, Inspiration, matters of honour and sacrifice. The realm of pure spirit. This realm can be accessed through the rune **Gebo**. Psychological attribute: Individuation.

2 *Vanaheim,* the realm of feelings; ruled by the Vanir, the gods of fertility, pleasure, peace and prosperity, all matters of eroticism and relationships. The element of Water. This realm can be accessed through the rune **Inguz**. Gods to call on for access to this very pleasant realm are *Freyr* and *Freyja*. Psychological attribute: Feeling.

3 *Lightalfheim,* realm of the light alfar, spirits of Air, all mental activities, art, creativity, plants and trees. Ruled over by *Freyr*. Access rune: **Sowulo**. Psychological attribute: thinking.

These are the three Upper Worlds, which can be accessed through pathwork and guided meditation using the given rune as a doorway; also power can be invoked from that realm through the associated rune.

The next three are the three Middle worlds. The first two, Muspelheim and Nifelheim, generated all of the other worlds.

4 *Muspelheim,* the realm of fire. Together with Nifelheim, a source of eternal creation through the interactions of their respective elements, Fire and Frost. Muspelheim is inhabited by the sons of *Surt*, who at the Ragnarok will destroy Midgard. A very hostile world; no travelling attempts have ever been recorded. For those who want to tempt wyrd, **Dagaz** is the ruling rune. For the purpose of divination, however, we focus upon the creative aspect of Muspelheim and allocate this word the psychological attribute of intuition.

5 *Nifelheim,* like Muspelheim, its polar opposite, is a very hostile world. It is ruled by an all-devouring serpent: *Niddhog*, the eater of the evil dead and drinker of blood. Nifelheim is a realm

of fog and mists, it is the realm of the shadow side of the unconscious; again a no-go area, the rune belonging with it is, not surprisingly, **Nauthiz**. Psychological attribute: Shadow.

6 *Midgard*, the realm of humanity, the inhabited world, civilization. Its guardian and protector is *Thor*. The rune connected with it is **Jera**. In psychological terms, this world represents the ordinary waking consciousness, the Ego or Mundane self.

Now we come to the Under Worlds.

7 *Swartalfheim*, the realm of the Inner Earth, the domain of the dwarves, who deal with precious metals and stones, working smithcraft: taking base materials and transforming them into higher materials, by means similar to alchemy. Their ruler is *Modsognir* and the rune that will grant access is **Eihwaz**. The psychological attribute is: sensation.

8 *Jotunheim*, realm of the frost giants, raw disruptive male power. This realm is tricky and confusing, it contains the realm of *Utgard Loki*, a King of Giants who cheats Thor by trickery and sorcery. The access rune is **Isa**. In this realm, nothing is as it appears; however, those well versed in shamanic travelling should be able to go there. For this reason I have assigned to this realm the Jungian psychological concept of the Animus, the male part of the self.

9 *Hel*, the realm of Hella, the goddess of death, counterpart of Odin in this respect. Odin shares the heroic dead with Freyja. The heroic dead are those warriors who have fallen in battle, and who in life were devoted to a specific God or Goddess, and may hope to share their realm with this deity after death. All others go to Hella's realm, a recycling plant for reincarnation. This realm can be travelled to quite safely provided certain precautions are taken. A pathworking to access this realm will be provided in chapter 6 on runes and magic. The realm of Hella can be accessed to communicate with ancestors and obtain knowledge from the dead. The access-rune is **Hagalaz**. Psychological attribute: Anima, female part of the self.

You will have noticed that Asgard, Midgard and Hel are connected linearly. I am very pleased with the result of this diagram as it is actually an improvement on the earlier one given in *Leaves of Yggdrasil* and repeated in *Northern Mysteries and Magic*. Thank you Odin!

All the access runes provided are non-invertible which means they are completely neutral in terms of positive or negative; they function purely from an impersonal perspective as keys to power — indeed, they might be called the nine 'songs of power'. Each one can mediate energy and information from their respective realm.

Example of a Nine Words Spread

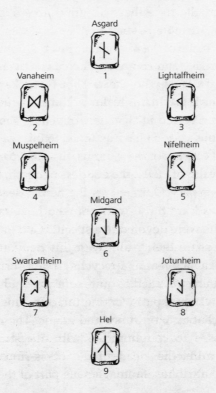

Asgard
1

Vanaheim
2

Lightalfheim
3

Muspelheim
4

Nifelheim
5

Midgard
6

Swartalfheim
7

Jotunheim
8

Hel
9

This is a type of reading which is suitable for an in-depth analysis of the various psychologcal functions in an individual and how they balance out. It is not necessary to ask specific questions. In this sample reading, the runes are:

Asgard:	Nauthiz	
Vanaheim:	Dagaz	
Lightalfheim:	Thurisaz	*inverted*
Muspelheim:	Berkana	*inverted*
Nifelheim:	Sowulo	
Midgard:	Laguz	*inverted*
Swartalfheim:	Perthro	*inverted*
Jotunheim:	Ansuz	*inverted*
Hel:	Algiz	*inverted*

For interpretation, one views the runes in connection with the three levels in turn. Examining the runes in the three Upperwolds we see that only Dagaz is in a favourable position. Nauthiz in Asgard is not favourable and neither is Thurisaz inverted in Lightalfheim. When interpreting, one has to develop the art of sensing which runes are compatible with which world and how they may affect each other. Nauthiz in Asgard means in this reading that the person is not yet or is not at this moment on-line with the forces and intelligences of Asgard. Lightalfheim, too, is inaccessible as there is a negative Thurisaz blocking any influences for this realm. Dagaz, the rune of Dawn and enlightenment in Vanaheim, the word of Vanir, states clearly that from this realm help can be sought and inspiration obtained — perhaps in the form of artistic endeavours. More could be said about this but space is limited.

Turning to the middle-worlds, we find Berkana inverted in Muspelheim. Obviously, in the context of this particular reading, this realm is hostile to creative forces represented by

Berkana, and therefore Berkana appears inverted. Nifelheim contains Sowulo, indicating that this realm can be of help. Since Nifelheim, amongst other things, represents the darkest, unacknowledged aspects of the personal subconscious as well as being a foggy place, Sowulo provides a redeeming factor. The sun can drive the fog away and shine her light on the amassed negative garbage in the subconscious. From this, practical knowledge can be obtained and unpleasant, 'forgotten', traumatic memories can be accessed, processed, assimilated and transmuted to positive power, through meditation on the relationship between Sun and the Shadow. Midgard has Laguz inverted; this suggests feelings of loss and disappointment in a worldly matter, a let-down by a loved one, being 'ripped off' or deceived; perhaps tears. This says you have to get in touch with your feelings, perhaps sort things out in a confrontation before you can let go and move on.

Moving on to the three Underworld runes, we come to Perthro inverted in Swartalfheim. Swartalfheim is the world of hidden treasure and Perthro is the rune of hidden mysteries and unexpected windfalls — but since it is inverted, there is nothing to expect from this combination. No access. In Jotunheim we find a situation of conflicting perspectives. Ansuz, the rune of Odin representing, amongst other things, communication, appears inverted. Aesir and Giants are opposing forces as we know, and this combination tells me that a row is about to ensue. The advice is, be very careful with any form of communication, keep your mouth shut for the moment and don't put anything in writing; there is a clear danger of abuse. Finally, we come to the inverted Algiz in Hella's realm. While its upright form indicates the tree of life, Algiz inverted is the symbol of the tree of death. This combination is not entirely negative, however. The advice offered is to seek the counsel of your elders who went before, ask for protection. Information is available, call on your ancestors and watch your dream space as it is likely that they will respond through this.

This is quite a comprehensive reading, and my interpretation is condensed by necessity into a few paragraphs. It is given as an example to experiment with. The only way to become proficient with this as well as any other type of reading is through practice and hard work. Always keep records and give yourself marks; review the record at least once a year to assess your progress. The interpretations I have given for the above reading are not fixed hard and fast: play about with it and the sooner you can dispense with this interpretation offered by me as an example, and develop your own, the better you will become at reading the runes.

For a casting cloth I can recommend a traditional design, and the above attributes allocated to the nine words can be applied:

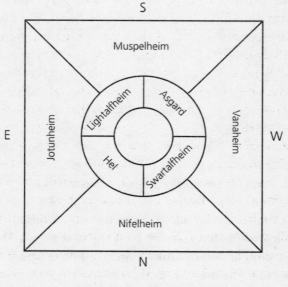

A Traditional Casting Cloth

This cloth can be used to cast the runes, and I suggest the following method. First, spread the cloth over a table. Then hold all the runes in a vessel: a cup, a beaker, a horn, etc. Invoke the three Norns saying 'Urd, Verdandi, Skuld', and throw the runes onto the cloth. Discount any runes which fall outside the cloth and view the others where they have fallen, interpreting them against the backdrop of the space they each occupy. For example, Dagaz falling in Asgard suggests a sudden spiritual awakening.

3. A YEARLY FORECAST

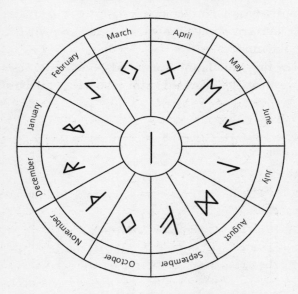

Example of a Yearly Forecast

The best time to do a yearly forecast is at the beginning of the year, which will help you to plan for the year ahead. This forecast, for example, was done on 1 January 1999. The dominating rune, placed in the centre of the spread to represent the querent, is Isa. The monthly runes are as follows:

January	Berkana	
February	Eihwaz	
March	Jera	
April	Gebo	
May	Ehwaz	
June	Teiwaz	*inverted*
July	Laguz	*inverted*
August	Dagaz	
September	Fehu	*inverted*
October	Inguz	
November	Thurisaz	*inverted*
December	Raido	

Isa in the centre means that the person concerned is stuck in a situation, at the time of the reading, and has been for about three months prior to this (this timing is because of Isa's connection with winter), with limited opportunity to move in a desired direction. The basic issue may be job related, but it may also affect other areas of life since the personal web of wyrd is a holistic concept.

January starts very well with a new opportunity, possibly leading to a new job, enterprise or any new project. Eihwaz in February adds some tension to this and an effort has to be made to prove oneself. In March a positive result arising from something originating a year beforehand (Jera meaning harvest or year) may come to the fore, possibly leading to the settling or signing of an agreement, with Gebo in April. This may involve finances; for instance, it could indicate the recovering of money owed. In May one may meet another person and invest hopes in a possible relationship; this, however, will not come to anything with Teiwaz inverted in June, as the person concerned is not what he or she pretended to be initially. As a consequence, there will be some sadness and regret in July with

Laguz inverted. August, with Dagaz, is the optimum time for a holiday. There is the danger of overspending on this with the result that in September, with Fehu inverted, there is a financial restraint or loss. In October, however, this should restore itself and something which started in April with the signing of a deal will pay off and come to fruition. November is the month where one has to watch one's health and energies, and attempt to avoid any conflicts and postpone possible disputes to December when, with Raido, one stands a better chance of obtaining a positive outcome.

This is an example made up with no real querent involved. It is given to show how one can read the runes in connection with the following runes, in a sequence, according to the yearly cycle. One can use the same reading to pick out issues which will influence the coming year as a whole, without necessarily including the months. To do this one looks at runes opposite and at right angles or in triangular formations with other runes.

Like this: Jera opposite Fehu inverted, squared 90 degrees by Teiwaz inverted, which is opposite Raido, which therefore also squares Jera and Fehu. This suggests a possible complicated legal situation, with a mixed result or an undecided result for that year, ie litigation, which could go on for some time, and involving financial costs. This is one example of how to connect runes in a pattern and draw a conclusion from this. Those of you familiar with astrology have an obvious advantage, but anyone can learn this if they put the effort in.

Let's look at the same runes divorced from the yearly cycle and instead using the twelve segments as the twelve houses derived from astrology. Those who have their own horoscope can overlay this with runes as an exercise and try to do a reading from this. The object of giving readings is assisting people in their life's situations to the best of one's ability, and anything that can add to this can and should be used. In fact, the twelve-house system is already very popular in combination with rune reading. Those who want to limit themselves to Norse symbolism exclusively can always re-name the houses after the twelve palaces of Asgard (see appendix).

The runes are read anti-clockwise from the first house. For those totally unfamiliar with the attributes of the houses I will give short definitions of these.

First house: the self; basic personality, how others perceive you, psychological motivation, ambitions, all beginnings, self-image and self-expression.

Second house: security, money, natural talents, material values, personal possessions.

Third house: early education, peers, siblings and relatives, short journeys, communication ability.

Fourth house: childhood environment, influence of the mother, physiological foundations, domestic issues.

Fifth house: luck, pleasure, children, love, creativity.

Sixth house: health, employment, service.

Seventh house: the other, spouse, partnerships, relationships. Opponents.

Eighth house: Transformation, sex, death, regeneration.

Ninth house: spiritual ambitions, philosophy, religion, higher education, long journeys.

Tenth house: career, public image, social contributions, authority, influence of the father.

Eleventh house: ideals, friendships, groups, social values and aspirations. Hopes and wishes.

Twelfth house: Endings, enemies' constraints, wyrd, past lives. Subconscious and sacrifices.

Let's attempt to interpret the previous runes on this model. Isa remains in the centre, representing, in this context, the situation as it is.

Example of an Astrological Forecast

First House: Berkana. Pleasant personal appearance and demeanour, this person is well-liked and appreciated by his or her peers. A gentle disposition, possible problem with assertiveness. Must develop persistence in any project.

Second house: Raido. A well-defined sense of fairness and what is right, a balanced view concerning finances and possessions. Possibly in the position to offer advice to others regarding these subjects.

Third house: Thurisaz (inverted). Not enough self-preservation. Must learn to say No. Tendency to avoid confrontation at the expense of self.

Fourth house: Inguz. Stable home background, perhaps too protected by the mother; must be more independent. Tend to rely too much on other people's opinion.

Fifth house: Fehu inverted. Tends to be too optimistic financially and has to avoid gambling or taking risks with money. Also must develop more self-esteem based on own observation, not other people's views.

Sixth house: Dagaz. A worry is to be resolved; a possible fear relating to health is unfounded, possibly a sudden improvement in employment opportunity.

Seventh house: Laguz. Possibly emotionally too dependent on partner; however, very loving in nature.

Eighth house: Teiwaz (inverted). A happening which may result in having to face death in one form or another, possibly an elder in the family. A confrontation with death which forces one to contemplate one's own mortality. *This does not mean the querent dies.*

Ninth house: Ehwaz. Idealistic approach and a positive outlook in life; an optimistic personal philosophy. This would be a good time to seek out like-minded people and/or explore alternative religions.

Tenth house: Gebo. An accomplishment in career, a promotion and possibly acceptance of a contract leading to a position in management.

Eleventh house: Jera. All good things are returned; also the not-so-good things albeit fewer in number. The returns are through other people and social acquaintances as well as personal friends.

Twelfth house: Eihwaz. An unusual experience leading to insight into a past event, possibly ancestral knowledge, the emergence of past life awareness. A possible personal sacrifice.

The above reading is very general and is offered to show how one may interpret the runes, by synthesizing the meaning of the runes with the meaning of the houses. In the first reading involving these runes, Laguz was interpreted as being inverted, in the second Laguz is interpreted as upright, this is because if one views the wheel of the year the runes move sunwise, and in the second reading with the houses the runes move anti-clockwise.

4. THE CROSS SPREAD

This spread is very useful where the querent needs help making either – or decisions, but it can also answer more complicated questions and solve problems.

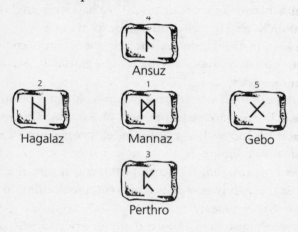

A Cross Spread

Here I have a simple spread which looks at the questions from five different angles. I have allocated runes to each square, and each rune conveys the interpretative meaning of the square.

One is Mannaz, the person who asks the question. The rune turning up here states where this person is coming from; it may relate to the subject matter of the question and in rare events may actually convey that it isn't the right question to ask or the right time to ask the question.

Two is Hagalaz: everything related to this question which arises from the immediate past, what gave rise to the need to ask the question. What went before.

Three is Perthro: gives information about an unseen or hidden aspect related to the question, it may point out something one had overlooked or was not aware of. What is behind this, or what is hidden from sight.

Four is Ansuz: gives a higher spiritual dimension in the light of the question and may show what spiritual forces are involved. It may also offer advice from the god/desses. What is above.

Five is Gebo: this should give the answer, interpreted in conjunction with the other four runes. You should now have an accurate response or advice regarding a question or problem.

This reading can be extended as follows. The method is the same as with the Nine Worlds spread. Select runes unseen on each of the squares; turn them over one by one, interpreting each one in turn, and then connect them to draw a far more detailed conclusion. Of course one can draw two or three runes for each square instead of one; this may give more elaborate information but it is also more difficult to interpret. However, as with all the above techniques, experimentation will generate experience.

THE USE OF RUNES
FOR PERSONAL
EMPOWERMENT,
SELF-DEVELOPMENT
AND RELATIONSHIP
COUNSELLING

n this chapter we are looking at how runes can help you to improve your personal life, relationships and circumstances, through understanding and growth.

SELF-ANALYSIS THROUGH THE RUNES

Runes can be employed periodically as a means of psychological exploration, to assess one's own strengths and weaknesses. For this purpose, I will extend the meaning of the runes from divination into psychotherapeutic applications, both for individuals and to offer a technique to explore the dynamics in a relationship. This goes further than the traditional methods of divination, but in this book I attempt to strike a balance between tradition and innovation.

The meanings of the runes given for this exercise are derived from their general meanings as given in chapter 2, but more specifically adapted to the purpose of psychology. The runes, projected at a more complicated level of depth psychology, will not change their essential nature. The runes may change their 'octave' but not their 'ground-tone'. For example, Fehu, in the mundane sense, means wealth and money prospects, whereas the same rune in a psychological reading means creative energies, in particular the level of self-confidence and self-esteem available to the querent, which allow him to improve his life's circumstances. The more one meditates on and experiments with these creative variations within the runes, the more inner resonance one will develop; thereby establishing a working relationship with the runes.

The basic meanings of the runes of the first aett to be applied in this type of consultation are listed below.

Fehu: Personal strength, attitude and expectations regarding money. Self-esteem and confidence.

Uruz: Instinctual drives versus personal discipline; raw force, physical health, endurance and assertiveness.

Thurisaz: The power of self-assertion and non-destructive confrontation with others. The individual's will and the opposing willpower from others.

Ansuz: Communication skills, the ability to adequately express oneself. The ability to listen to others, leadership qualities. Higher sources of communications, from either within or outside the self.

Raido: The ability to realize right from wrong and the power to base your decisions on this. The amount of control that the individual can exert in his or her life.

Kenaz: The ability to recognize a situation for what it is, to be objective and apply common sense. The individual's knowledge and capacities.

Gebo: The ability to compromise, to give and receive in equal

measure. The individual's attitude towards giving and receiving.

Wunjo: The ability to relax and enjoy oneself, sense of humour. The individual's potential for enjoyment and his or her chances of being successful.

Hagalaz: How the past may be exerting its influence on the present, and how to use this for change.

Nauthiz: The need to recognize one's limitations and to either accept or transform these.

Isa: Areas one prefers not to look into, possible suppressed memories, which have to be assimilated. Blockages, frustrations and hindrances.

Jera: What one may expect to occur as a result from previous actions. The time factor in the individual's development.

Eihwaz: What one fears, either in objective terms or subjectively, and the ability to achieve one's desires; tensions between fear and desires.

Perthro: That which is hidden and ready to emerge. The ability of introspection and self-awareness.

Algiz: Matters of self-protection and self-preservation. The ability to defend oneself and protect one's own.

Sowulo: The source within, which guides the individual on his or her path.

Teiwaz: The ability of objective judgement and fairness; the potential for handling a conflict correctly; warrior attitudes and courage.

Berkana: Creative abilities, nurturing and birth processes in the self.

Ehwaz: Emotional responses, adaptability and subjectivity.

Mannaz: The mind and intellectual objectivity.

Laguz: The intuitive faculties and the potential for sympathetic feelings.

Inguz: The potential for individuation and integration.

Othala: The relatedness to heritage and kin, and awareness of
   origins.
Dagaz: The ultimate aim of transformation of the personal consciousness into whatever one envisages being the greater
   whole.

The beginner may find it helpful if an example of a reading
using this technique is given in detail. We use here a 'futhark
spread', in which the querent selects all of the runes, one at a
time; these are laid out in futhark order, in three rows of eight,
so that their positions each correspond to one of the runes of the
futhark. The following is a description of a profile reading for a
middle-aged professional female, who anticipated some trouble
in her personal and professional life. As the reading below
clearly shows, most of the perceived trouble was in her own
mind in the form of fear, anxiety and some depression, without
actually any indication of major disasters about to happen. It is
in such circumstances that a psychological profile reading can
be very helpful as it mostly points out subjective realities.

Fehu pairs with: *Gebo* — A very positive combination, meaning
   that she may expect a monetary gift, possibly as a reward.
Uruz pairs with: *Isa* — Must watch her health and examine her
   diet.
Thurisaz pairs with: *Jera* — Possible repercussions of an argument or a falling out last year.
Ansuz pairs with: *Hagalaz* — Negative feedback possible: malicious gossip and severe criticism by an elder person.
Raido pairs with: *Dagaz* — A decisive move will have a positive
   change as a result.
Kenaz pairs with: *Eihwaz* — understanding has to precede the
   taking of any risk.

Gebo pairs with: *Kenaz inverted* — Cannot see how well off she really is; must look more on the bright side.

Wunjo pairs with: *Wunjo inverted* — A lack of enjoyment or pessimistic outlook, which she can change herself by being aware that she creates her own reality. By changing her negative expectation, she may alter her wyrd in this respect.

Hagalaz pairs with: *Teiwaz* — She must take decisive action to break with certain aspects of her emotional past and move on, possibly in a completely different direction.

Nauthiz pairs with: *Sowulo* — Again the need to seek the sun, ie to cultivate a more positive outlook and approach.

Isa pairs with: *Ansuz inverted* — This is a major block in her psyche; perhaps outside advice is required.

Jera pairs with: *Othala inverted* — Excessive anxiety that she may lose her home in a year's time, but she can take action right now to prevent this.

Eihwaz pairs with: *Mannaz* — She must maintain her integrity within a small group of people and not be persuaded or coerced by majority opinion if this is not in her own best interest.

Perthro pairs with: *Perthro inverted* — This area is closed off for now.

Algiz pairs with: *Inguz* — She can expect protection and nurturing within her family and would probably do well to forge closer bonds with some of them.

Sowulo pairs with: *Uruz* — She must balance fire (yang) and ice (yin) to counteract the above effect of Uruz paired with Isa. The Chinese concepts of Yin and Yang correspond very neatly to 'fire' and ice'. Spend more time outdoors.

Teiwaz pairs with: *Laguz* — A balance has to be struck between justice and mercy. She must be less rigid with implementing the rules and be more understanding of other people's failings.

Berkana pairs with: *Fehu inverted* — A creative project may have to be shelved due to lack of funds.

Ehwaz pairs with: *Raido inverted* — She must not follow advice given by people around her but follow her own instincts for now.

Mannaz pairs with: *Thurisaz* — She must not give in to pressure from other people attempting to persuade her in a certain direction, by decisively cutting ties where and when needed.

Laguz pairs with: *Ehwaz* — She has to use her intuition to distinguish between true and false friends, and consider her own interest a bit more.

Inguz pairs with: *Berkana inverted* — She has to consolidate what she's got and for the moment be content with this; any premature attempt to expand will meet with failure.

Othala pairs with: *Algiz* — She must ward her home, and secure her position within it.

Dagaz pairs with: *Nauthiz* — For the moment, lay off any heavy occult work.

So, that is that. As this reading is not specifically bound to any given time it seems that some of it was already known to the client, and was applicable in the immediate past; some of it seems to give caution in the near future. This is the only weak point of this type of reading; it is very difficult to pin it down timewise. It seems to give a wide-angle snapshot of the 'now' — with the immediate past and present included! The art here is to intuitively feel which is which. The lady concerned contacted me today ten days after the reading and we went over it again and since then she has noticed things happening in her surroundings which where clearly indicated in the reading. Looking at it with hindsight proved most interesting: virtually everything fell into place and very specifically so. Perhaps it is a good idea to do this type of reading once a month and then read back every week and review it. It seems from the above reading and the subsequent events in the lady's life that some of the information provided by the reading pertained to the immediate past — perhaps even from a few weeks previously — and some of it materialized virtually the same week! That's quite exceptional, but it does prove the validity of this type of reading.

PARTNERSHIP READING

The next technique I developed was for the purpose of exploring areas within a relationship and creating opportunities to discuss, iron out, and prevent or deal with any possible problems which may occur at any time in any relationship. To utilize this reading technique, however, the relationship must be basically strong. Both partners must be totally honest and trusting with each other, as areas of vulnerability could be exposed and therefore exploited. It works in a similar way to synastry astrology, although it is easier and faster. Each rune is interpreted to refer to a specific area of a relationship between people in keeping with the rune's basic meaning. For this technique to work, both partners must be present and each must have a set of runes. A cloth is made portraying all the twenty-four runes and arranged either in a circle or in a straight line.

The following is an example. The first rune on the cloth is Fehu, which represents the financial prospects in the relationship and the attitude of both partners towards finance. Both partners select a rune unseen and place it on each side of Fehu. The rune-reader turns the runes over and interprets them in the light of the Fehu rune. If, for example, the first partner draws Gebo and the second Nauthiz, it could be the case that the second partner regards the first one as having too generous or irresponsible an attitude towards money and security within the relationship, whereas the first partner may well take the view that the other is too restrictive with finance and too afraid to take risks. Clearly this could give rise to an area of possible conflict. By being aware of potential problems, they can work together to reach a compromise in the matter.

Below are listed the meanings of the runes adapted to the framework of personal relationships.

Fehu: The financial prospect in this relationship and the attitudes of the partners towards money, sharing wealth.

Uruz: Endurability and strength of the relationship.

Thurisaz: General conflict area; battle of wills, outside disruptive influences.

Ansuz: Communication within and about the relationship.

Raido: The rights of each individual within the relationship.

Kenaz: Learning and teaching from and with each other.

Gebo: Giving and taking.

Wunjo: Enjoyment, and fun, shared sense of humour.

Hagalaz: Unconscious influences operating within the relationship; past experiences in other relationships, including projections from parents.

Nauthiz: Areas of restriction; possessiveness; mutual needs.

Isa: Privacy; those areas in the relationship that are not shared.

Jera: Long- or short-term influences upon each other.

Perthro: Hidden aspects within the relationship, secrets.

Eihwaz: Ideals; expectations, and disappointments thereof.

Algiz: Caring and protecting.

Sowulo: Maintaining one's individuality within the relationship.

Teiwaz: Combined strength; authority; who is the boss?

Berkana: Fertility; children; parental projection of the self onto the children.

Ehwaz: Sexuality; any joint efforts; adaptability, tolerance.

Mannaz: Intellectual compatibility and mutual understanding. Shared ideas.

Laguz: Empathic, affectionate, emotionality, loving.

Inguz: Family matters, parents and children.

Othala: Home life, property, 'in-laws', social life.

Dagaz: Contributions to each other's well being, growth and change.

To experiment with this reading I reiterate, one must be willing to face unpleasant truths without, however using the reading to cast blame.

This type of reading can also be adapted to a business partnership. In that case, just adapt the given meaning of the runes above for a personal relationship to less emotional interpretations.

RUNES AND MAGIC

R unes always were and still are used for magical workings. In popular culture, this magical aspect of the runes
has long been seen as dark and sinister — as, for
instance, in M.R. James' classic horror story, which was made
into the film *Night of the Demon*. Central to the story is a traditional method of planting a curse using runes, employed by
a magician whose character was supposedly modelled on
Aleister Crowley! The truth is, however, that the runes are more
commonly used for constructive magical purposes, such as
healing and helping. Sometimes a more aggressive working is
needful; I myself only have done a destructive working once,
back in 1983, when my life was being threatened. It worked,
quite dramatically, but succeeded also in terrifying me — and
everyone else living in the house at the time. Generally speaking, aggressive workings are best avoided unless absolutely
necessary, both on ethical and common sense grounds; negativ-
ity has a habit of bouncing back!

To work magic with runes one has to work with the
gods, whatever one perceives them to be. Their existence,
be it subjective or objective in your interpretation, has to be
assumed as a working paradigm. It is really of no consequence
whether these gods and goddesses live in your own head, in the

collective unconscious or on Mars for that matter. What is of consequence is that when working magic with the runes one is aware that one is accessing forces *behind* the runes; namely, what we call the 'gods' or 'archetypes' if you prefer.

So let's introduce the main gods and their associated runes in order of prominence and relevance to magic. For a more in-depth description of these gods and others I refer the reader to my earlier book, *Northern Mysteries and Magic*.

THE GODS AND GODDESSES AND THE RUNES

Since there are so many different forms of several of our deities' names, and since this is a simple introduction, for the ease of the newcomer I have chosen to use the Anglicized Norse forms which are best known to most people.

THE HIGH GODS

Odin: Originally a god of death, whose range later came to encompass magic (especially runic magic), battle (giving victory by choosing who should die), and poetry.

Odin won the runes by hanging on a tree for nine days and nights, wounded with his own spear. He gave up one of his eyes for a drink from the Well of Mimir ('Memory'). To his chosen ones, he gives victory, inspiration, magic, madness and death when he sees fit. He is seen especially as a god of wisdom, a patron of poets, thinkers and singers.

Odin usually appears as a grey-bearded man, tall and thin, with a blue-black cloak and an eye-patch or wide-brimmed hat tilted to hide his missing eye. His weapon is the casting spear Gungnir, with which he dooms his chosen ones to die in battle. He has two wolves, Geri and Freki (both names mean 'the Greedy'); two ravens, Huginn ('the Thoughtful') and Muninn ('the Mindful') and a grey, eight-legged horse called Sleipnir ('Slipper'). He is the husband of Frigga and the father of many gods and human heroes. As the leader of the Wild Hunt, he also brings fruitfulness to the fields.

Odin is a god of foresight, careful weaving of plots, and long-term agendas.

Associated Runes: Ansuz, Gebo, Wunjo, Eihwaz, Othala, Dagaz.

Thor: 'Thunder', son of Odin and Earth. The most popular god of the Viking Age, and often known now as 'god of the common man'. Thor appears as a big, muscular man with red hair and beard and huge fiery eyes. He drives a wagon which is drawn by two goats, Tanngrísnir (Teeth-Barer or Teeth-Gnasher) and Tanngnjóstr (Tooth-Gritter). His weapons are his hammer, Mjolnir, and his belt of strength.

Associated Runes: Thurisaz, Uruz, Raido, Sowulo.

Freya: Freya is probably the best-known and best-loved of the goddesses today. Her title simply means 'Lady'; her original name is not known. Freya is the 'wild woman' among the deities of the North: free with her sexual favours (though furious when an attempt is made to marry her off against her will); mistress of Odin and several other gods and men; skilled in the form of ecstatic, consciousness-altering, and sometimes malicious magic called seidhr; and chooser of half the slain on the battlefield (Odin gets the other half).

Freya's chief attribute is the necklace called Brisingamen, which she bought from four dwarves at the price of four nights of her love. This goddess drives a wagon drawn by two cats, perhaps large forest-cats such as lynxes, and is seen today as the patron goddess of cats and those who keep them.

Associated Runes: Fehu, Perthro, Hagalaz, Berkana, Laguz.

Frey: 'Frey' is a title simply meaning 'Lord'; his original name was apparently some form of Yngvi/Ing. Together with Thor, Frey was one of the best-loved gods of the Viking Age. His holy animal was the boar.

Frey was called for frith (fruitful peace) at home, and for good weather and gentle rains. He was, and is, often thought of as a giver of riches, whose blessing is called on for fruitfulness and growth in all fields of endeavour.

Associated Runes: Jera, Ehwaz, Inguz.

Frigga: Wife of Odin, Frigga is the patron goddess of the home and of the mysteries of the married woman. She is seen as Odin's match (and sometimes his better) in wisdom; she shares his high-seat, from which they look out over the worlds together.

Frigga is especially concerned with keeping social order. She is called on for blessings when women are giving birth and for help in matters of traditional women's crafts (spinning, weaving, cooking, sewing) and the magics worked thereby. Frigga can also be called on by mothers who want to protect their children.

Frigga is the mother of Balder, and is often thought of as still mourning for him. She is a seeress, who knows all fates, though she seldom speaks of them.

Associated Runes: Perthro, Berkana.

Tyr: His name simply means 'god'; at one time, he may have been the Germanic equivalent of Zeus or Jupiter, the 'Sky-Father' of the Indo-Europeans. In Old Norse, Tyr appears only in the myth in which he gives up his hand so that the gods can bind the Wolf Fenrir. However, there are strong suggestions that he may originally have been a god of justice.

Associated Runes: Teiwaz, Raido, Gebo.

HeimdallR: Watcher at the gates of Asgard, he can hear the grass growing on the ground and the wool on a sheep's back, and needs no sleep. He came to Midgard in order to father the three tribes of humans — thralls, freemen and rulers — and to teach runes and lore to the last. Heimdall is sometimes seen as a rather aloof god and lacking in humour; however, he is a great teacher, and an especially good god to call on for those who work in subjects calling for cool intellect rather than the furious inspiration given by Odin.

Associated Runes: Algiz, Mannaz, Dagaz.

OTHER GOD/DESSES AND WIGHTS

Austri, Sudri, Vestri, Nordri: The four dwarves who hold up the four corners of the sky (Ymir's skull). Sometimes also thought to be the four who forged Freya's necklace Brisingamen. Their names in Old Norse — Austri, Sudri, Vestri and Nordri — mean East, South, West and North respectively.

Runes to use on the quarters to invoke the powers are: East, Gebo; South, Dagaz; West, Inguz; North, Isa.

Balder: Son of Odin and Frigga. After his death was foretold, Frigga persuaded everything in the Nine Worlds to swear not to harm him, but neglected the mistletoe, which she thought was too small and weak. Making a game of his invulnerability, the gods cast weapons at him; meanwhile, Loki made an arrow of mistletoe and put it in the hand of Balder's blind brother Hodur, aiming it for him.

Associated Rune: Sowulo.

Loki: A giant brought among the Aesir by Odin, who swore blood-brotherhood with him, Loki wavers between a culture-hero/Trickster and a destroyer. He is responsible for getting the

gods most of their goods, but only after he has led them to the edge of destruction. Loki also brings a surprising amount of humour into the Norse tales. As well as being the father of the Wolf Fenrir, the Midgard Serpent and, allegedly, Hel, he is also the mother of Odin's eight-legged horse Sleipnir, and cross-dresses in the typically feminine falcon-hides of Frigga and Freyja when he needs to fly between the worlds.

Associated Rune: Dagaz.

Eir: Goddess of healing, patroness of health-care workers, called on against sickness or injury. She is one of the goddesses on the mountain called Lyfia ('to heal through magic'), and gives both physical and psychic means of healing; shamanic healing, especially, falls into her realm.

Associated Runes: Uruz; Jera; Laguz.

Hel: Ruler of the kingdom of death. The Prose Edda describes her as half-black, half-white (she is sometimes seen as half-rotting, half alive) and of grim and unmistakable appearance. There is no evidence for the worship of the goddess Hel in elder times, but there are several folk who work with her today. Also called Hella.

Associated Runes: Hagalaz, Eihwaz.

Holda: A goddess known through German folklore, her name means 'the Gracious One'. I think she is a friendlier form of Hella, or Hel; however, she has also much in common with Frigga, being the patroness of spinners and the keeper of social order, especially enforcing taboos about working on holy days. She is also said to be the keeper of the souls of unbaptized (or sometimes simply young) children, and women who want to bear children ask for them at her well. Holda also appears at times as the leader of the Wild Hunt. According to one tale, it was she who

taught humans how to plant and process flax. When it snows,
Holda is supposed to be shaking out her feather-bed.

Associated Runes: Hagalaz, Perthro, Berkana.

Idunna: the goddess who keeps the apples of youth, by which
the gods stay ever-young. Apples are one of the oldest and holiest symbols of life and rebirth among the Germanic folk,
appearing as grave-gifts from the Bronze Age onward.

Associated Runes: Jera, Berkana, Inguz.

Land-wights: The beings who dwell in rocks, springs and so
forth. They are shy and easily driven away (especially by noise
or strife and even more so by pollution); when they have fled,
the land will not prosper. In the mid-seventies some clairvoy-
ants in Holland saw the land-wights moving out over a rainbow bridge spanning the North Sea and moving into Sweden.
Since then the Dutch have cleaned up their act and apparently
the land-wights are moving back slowly. The land-wights are
friendly towards humans who treat them well. Gifts of food and
drink were often left by their dwelling places.

Associated Runes: Inguz, Jera.

Mimir: A giant, perhaps the brother of Odin's etin-mother
Bestla. Keeper of the Well of Mimir, in which all wisdom lies —
the spring where Odin gave up his eye to drink. Odin learned
the Nine Songs of Power from Mimir's head.

Associated Runes: Kenaz, Ansuz.

Nerthus: The 'Mother Earth' worshipped by the North Sea
Germans, according to the Roman historian Tacitus. Her worship included the springtime procession of a wagon which bore
her image about the countryside, finally arriving at a holy
island within a lake.

Associated Rune: Laguz.

Norns: The three Norns, Urd (Wyrd), Verdandi and Skuld, are etin-maidens who guard the Well of Urd from which the World-Tree springs. They reach into the Well's waters (the past) and sprinkle the Tree to shape the present and future. They are also said to do their shaping by cutting runes and/or by spinning and weaving.

Associated Runes: Hagalaz, Nauthiz, Isa, Jera, Perthro.

Skadi: Daughter of the giant Thjazi, who came among the Aesir in full armour to take revenge for her father. As part of her weregild, she demanded a husband; she had wanted Balder, but, being forced to choose among the gods by their feet alone, ended up with Njord. His sea-home was as unpleasant to her as her mountain-home was to him, and so they parted. She later bore a son to Odin. Skadi is a goddess of skiing, hunting, revenge, protection of the clan, and those women who follow the path of the 'Maiden Warrior'.

Associated Runes: Isa, Eihwaz, Teiwaz.

Valkyries: 'Choosers of the Slain', these maidens were originally seen as frightful battle-spirits accompanying Odin in his work of marking men for death in war. The most famous of the valkyries, known chiefly through Wagner's *Ring Cycle*, is Brunnhilde, demoted from her position for defending a hero against Odin's will and punished by being forced to fall in love with Siegfried the Dragon-Slayer.

Associated Rune: Algiz.

SOUL-LORE

Before we can explore magic from a specific Northern perspective we need to look at the metaphysical thoughts and concepts held by our ancestors. To work effective magic it is necessary to develop the various parts of the magical self. Our people had a fairly complex set of beliefs regarding the several parts which went to make up a human being. These parts are the physical body and the psychic part of the self usually called soul. The soul itself was thought to comprise various components which are listed below.

Fylgja — English equivalent *fetch* — a sort of Guardian spirit, usually embodied in an animal or human shape which reflects your inner nature. Wolves and bears were particularly common among the Northern folk, as the plethora of Germanic wolf/bear names suggest. The fetch is related to the shamanic 'totem animal' or 'power animal' or personal Norn. In other occult traditions such as Qabala and Thelema, the fylgja would be the Holy Guardian Angel, sometimes called the Higher Self. It attaches itself to the individual from birth, or more correctly from conception, and remains with the individual during its lifetime. It may then seek attachment to another member of the clan or family of the person. It is a being which mediates between Gods and humans.

Hamingja — close to the concept of *mana*, but also has a tenuous link to Wyrd and the Old Norse concept of luck. Hamingja is related to the deeds of ancestors and one's own behaviour in terms of the concept of honour. The hamingja is the personal magical power source and the shape-shifting force, the shape-shifting material being the *hamr* and the intent or will being part of the *hugr*. Another definition is 'luck' or 'fortune'. Like the fylgja, the hamingja is also seen as being a protective spiritual being and indeed differentiation between hamingja and fylgja is not always easy to determine.

Hamr — a subtle, plastic-like, image-forming material surrounding the physical body, roughly comparable with etheric material or ectoplasm. It can be used by the Hugr for shapeshifting and sending and can operate outside the physical body. It is used to leave the body during sleep or shamanic trance and can assume animal form. The idea of course is to train oneself magically to do this at will.

Hugr — the personality aspect of the soul, which is built up during a specific incarnation in a specific time and place and relates to that life alone. The term hugr is related to the name of one of Odin's raven, Huginn, which may mean 'the thoughtful' or 'the bold'. Mythology has it that Odin each day sent out his two ravens Huginn and Muninn so that they might return with information for him. Likewise it is possible with considerable effort to send one's hugr out to gain or retrieve knowledge from other realities or to perform workings. The hugr represent qualities which are now called thought, wish, desire and temperament. There is a strong connection between the hugr and the fylgja. In a sending or a shape-shift the matter is taken from the hamr and shaped at will, the will being an aspect of the hugr.

Minne — the several forms of memory — personal memory, ancestral memory, racial or folk memory. It twins with the hugr.

Much of Norse magic is concerned with the hugr, which is comparable with the Christian notion of the soul, but differs from it in an important respect. The soul is regarded as being a part of the godhead, whereas the hugr relates to the mental rather than spiritual life of the individual and manifests as personality, feelings, thoughts, desires, etc. Hugr and Minne are reminiscent of the left and right hemispheres of the brain.

Manipulation of the hugr is the real basis of magic, as will be demonstrated shortly. Being able to control the hugr not only places you firmly in control of yourself but enables you to safe-guard others. Instances are known of the uncontrolled hugr proving strong enough to affect animals and even other humans adversely. Nose itches? Ears ringing? Toe throbbing? Someone is thinking about you. Hiccough or tickling sensation? Same thing. What you're experiencing is the hugr of the person who is thinking of you impinging upon your physical body because they have not learned how to control it properly. Or, if they have, then the action must be regarded as deliberate and you must safeguard yourself when dealing with them.

MAGIC — TYPES AND DEFINITIONS

Magic has always been difficult to define, and virtually every school of magic defines it differently. The main problem is a compulsion to attempt a single definition which is all-purpose; this can only work for a single set of circumstances, not as a generality. We offer three main definitions of magic in the Northern tradition because the definition varies according to circumstances.

1 Practical or pragmatic magic — advancing materially. Magic is the art of manipulating the law of probabilities in your favour.
2 Personal magic — advancing psychologically. Magic is the art of knowing oneself through working with the mythology and inculcating the folk-soul and its precepts.
3 Devotional magic — advancing spiritually. Magic is the art of transmuting oneself into a being capable of conversing and interacting with the deities.

In the Northern Tradition two distinct branches of the magical art were in use: Galdr and Seidhr.

128   *Galdr* is the magic of charms, a mixture of poetry and sorcery. It has an implied acceptability for the peoples amongst whom it was found, certainly in pre-Christian times, though that acceptability doesn't imply a universal welcome, as is the case with magic almost universally. Galdr magic is more akin to the modern practice of ceremonial magic.

Seidhr, however, is both a complementary practice and an exact opposite. Whilst galdr is acceptable, seidhr is regarded with total anathema, despite its impeccable mythological origins. It positively reeks of antisocial and perverse behaviour. The reason is found in the Ynglinga Saga, where Odin's powers as the archetypal Norse magician are described. With his various galdr accomplishments, the author, Snorri Sturlusson, adds that Odin also understood the practices in which the most potent magic was to be found, and used them himself. Its purposes appear mostly dark grey by modern standards, if not positively black, and include foreknowledge of an individual's destiny, the imposition of death, illness, misfortune and bad luck, as well as the befuddlement of mind and bodily strength. In many respects seidhr is closely allied to shamanism, and both make use of trance states. I think the most compatible modern term to seidhr would be 'sorcery' in its darker meaning. The more positive prophetic aspect of seidhr nowadays, usually called spae-craft (see page 129), appears to be a form of mediumship, similar to spiritualism: the beings are called into the stead and entertained by the recital of a specific chant before they will reveal their knowledge of what shall come to pass.

    The difference in appreciation between those two traditional forms of Norse magic is a bit like the Victorian respectable Golden Dawn magician and the village witch! Another distinction is that galdr magic is used under the control of the will of the magician, with a specific intent.

The magical form known to our forebears as galdr is generally seen as the most characteristic form of Germanic magic, encompassing as it does both magical songs and the might of the runes. In contrast to seidhr and spae-craft, both of which are chiefly trance-oriented and involve a direct contact of the worker's soul with the Otherworld to affect the thoughts and spirits of others (seidhr) or receive prophetic wisdom (spae-craft), galdr is focused and directed within the Midgard by the conscious mind of the worker. Galdr is, by definition, a vocal magic: the word means literally 'song', and the connection between the noun *galdr* and the verb *gala*, 'to sing' (or: to croak or crow like a bird), was as obvious to our Norse forebears as to any modern etymologist. It may be observed that vocalization is an important part of most forms of magic, and that seidhr is also characterized by certain chants.

Closely related to seidhr is another magical, more spiritual practice, namely *Spae-Craft*. In the earlier days of our folk, the most honoured female leaders of the tribes were the spae-women who advised the war-chiefs concerning their battles with Rome. The most notable of these women was the Veleda, who foresaw the victory of the Batavi and gave advice for the tribe to rise against the Romans in 69 CE. Of her, Tacitus says, 'She was a maiden from the tribe of the Bructeri who possessed great powers, according to the old custom of the Germanic peoples to regard many women as seeresses, and in an extended superstition to consider them even to be goddesses'. (*Histories* IV, 61.)

Spae-craft is still practised today, it is a more communal form of magic in which whole communities participate, whereas both seidhr and galdr are practised in closed groups or solitary.

RUNIC COMBINATIONS FOR SPECIFIC MAGICAL PURPOSE

Runes can be combined in a sigil or symbol to synthesize their energies and these bind-runes are part of the magical practice. First, as always, one must develop a well-defined understanding of the meaning of runes as applied to magic. If you have read the foregoing chapters that should not be a problem. Second, one has to phrase exactly a statement of intent, outlining the objective of the working. It is best to do this in a poetic format, especially if a repetitive chant could be composed, ie a verbal spell to be recited over the bind-rune whilst it is constructed. Once, while living in a communal house, I was placed in a position where it became necessary to 'persuade' someone to leave. I constructed a runic sigil incorporating the person's name and a Raido rune to get him moving and, whilst beating a drum, simply chanted: 'Eeny, meeny, miny mo; Roger the lodger has to go!' He left at six o'clock the next morning! A simple repetitive spell, in rhyme, is all it takes. One might chant: 'Tip, tap, tob, I will get this job', just before an interview having combined the runes Eihwaz, Ansuz, Mannaz and Wunjo in a sigil drawn either on a runestave carried in a pouch around the throat (the throat chakra relates to communications) or else painted below one's collar.

EXAMPLE BIND-RUNES AND CHARMS

For travelling: ᚱᛖ or ᛖᚱ

    Suggested Runes: Raido, Ehwaz, (Laguz)

Safely I ride, safely I go,
Safe fare over road and foam,
Rightly beneath me all roads flow,
And whole come again to home.

Gladly ride I roads aright,
In faring fear no ill,
By Sun's warmth and Moon's soft light,
I fare, and find my fill.

For a job: ᛉᛈ or ᛚᛈ
  Suggested Runes: Eihwaz, Wunjo, Kenaz

The wheat grows fair in fields all,
The worker earns his/her pay,
The crafter hears keen tools' call,
I'll find fit work this day.

For healing: ᛏ
  Suggested Runes: Uruz, Jera, Sowulo, Laguz

By healing honey, herbs of strength,
By flood-tide's flowing roll,
By depths of sea and heaven's length,
Be body here made whole!

For wealth: ᚷ
  Suggested Runes: Fehu, Gebo, Kenaz

Fire of gold and field's grain,
The gifts of good all glow.
Upon my work shall weal rain,
Wealth to my winning flow.

For reconciliation or restoration of peace after a bad argument
with someone you would rather not lose permanently: ᛗᛏ
  Suggested Runes: Gebo, Wunjo, Ehwaz

No strife nor storm shall struggle on,
Our troubled times are past.
Bring friendship's ale forth from store,
And love return at last.

For losing excess weight (backing up a sensible diet, of course): ᚱ
   Suggested Runes: Uruz, Raido, Nauthiz

Lithe and slender, slim and light,
As birch at break of day,
My body shape with shining might,
And drop all dross away.

Bind-runes and charms can be constructed for any purpose, one only has to think runically, translating the objective in runic format. Often when constructing a bind-rune one 'gains' an extra rune. See for example the healing bind-rune which acquired an extra Teiwaz.

TECHNOLOGY OF RUNIC MAGIC

We now turn to the Rúnatál section of the poem called 'Hávamál' ('The Words of the High One') in the Elder Edda, which is spoken from the point of view of Odin himself. This poem is full of magical implications as we shall see when we look at the commentary.

I wot that I hung on the windy tree
  nights all nine,
wounded by spear, given to Ódhinn,
  given, self to myself,
on that tree of which no man knows
  where it rises from roots.

They comforted me not with loaf nor with horn,
  I pried below me,
took up the runes, screaming I took them,
  and fell back from there afterwards.

Fimbul-songs nine took I from the famous son
  of Bölthorn, Bestla's father,
and a drink I got of the dear mead,
  sprinkled from Ódhroerir.

I took to waxing fruitful and becoming wise,
  and grew and held myself well,
Word led me from word to another word,
work led me from work to another work.

You should find runes and read the staves,
  mickle great staves,
  mickle strong staves,
  which Fimbul-Thulr stained
  and the Ginn-Reginn readied,
  and Hroptr risted.

Ódhinn among Æsir, for the alfs, Dáinn,
    Dvalinn for the dwarves
    Ásvidhr for the etins,
    I risted some myself.

Know you, how to rist, know you, how to read?
Know you, how to colour, know you, how to test?
Know you, how to ask, know you, how to bless?
Know you, how to send, know you, how to sacrifice?

Better 'tis unoffered than to be over-offered,
    a gift ever looks for a gift;
better 'tis unsent than over-sacrificed,
So Thundr wrote before the history of folks,
there he rose up when he came again.

I know a song no folk-ruler's queen knows,
    nor human kinsman;
'Help' it hight, because it shall help,
against sicknesses and hurts and sorrows full-wrought.

That ken I secondly which men's sons need,
they who wish to live as healers.

That ken I third, if great need is on me,
    chains against my foe,
edges I deafen of shots against me,
    that those weapons cannot bite.

That ken I fourth, if are set upon me
    bonds upon my limbs,
so I chant that I can go,
fetters spring from my feet,
and chains spring from hands.

PRINCIPLES OF RUNES

That ken I fifth, if I see the shot on the way,
    throwing-spear in the folk's throng,
it cannot fly so fast that I cannot stop it,
    if I should sight it.

That ken I sixth, if some thane would scathe me,
    with a young root's wood,
I will be hale but who says he hates me,
    the harm eats him rather than me.

That ken I seventh if I see high fire,
    in the hall around my seat-kin,
It does not burn so broadly that I cannot protect from it,
    I know how to sing that galdr.

That ken I eighth which is for all,
    a needful thing to take.
Where hate waxes among warriors' sons,
    I am able to quell it.

That ken I ninth if there is need for me
    to save my ship on the flood,
I can still the wind upon the waves,
    and make all the sea to sleep.

That ken I tenth if I see garth-riders
    playing aloft
I can work it that the wild ones fare (home),
    their shapes home,
    their souls home.

PRINCIPLES OF RUNES

That ken I eleventh if I shall into battle
    lead old friends,
I sing under shield-rim that they fare with power,
    hale to the battle,
    hale from the battle,
    they come hale, where-ever.

That ken I twelfth if I see up on a tree
    a dangling hanged-man,
so I rist and in runes I colour,
    that so the man walks
    and speaks with me.

That ken I thirteenth if I shall cast water
    upon a young thane,
he shall not fall although he comes in battle,
    he shall not sink before swords.

That ken I fourteenth if I shall, before the folk,
    speak of the gods,
of Æsir and elves I can tell all,
    few unwise ones are so able.

That ken I fifteenth which Thjódhrørir sang,
    dwarf, before Delling's door.
Might sang he to Æsir, power to the elves,
    understanding to Ódhinn.

That ken I sixteenth if of a young maid I will
    have all heart and pleasure,
I turn the soul of the white-armed woman
    and wend to bed with her.

That ken I seventeenth that she will not scorn me
   for any other man —
this song remember you, Loddfáfnir,
   long will you lack it,
   but it will be good to you, if you get it,
   useful, if you take it,
   needful, if you receive it.

That ken I eighteenth which I will not make known,
   not to maid nor man's wife —
it is wholly better which one alone knows —
   that follows to the end of the song —
except for her who lies in my arms
   or be my sister.

Now are Hár's sayings spoken in the hall of Hár,
   all-needful for men's sons,
   un-needful for etins' sons.
Hail the one who spoke! Hail the one who knows!
   useful to the one who takes,
   help, to the one who heeds.

Translation from Old Norse by Dr Stephan Grundy PhD

RÚNATÁL (COMMENTARY)

The version of this portion of the 'Hávamál' given above clearly divides into at least two distinct sections, both of which are highly relevant for any understanding of Northern magic and runecraft. Our main concern here is with the list of charms, numbered 1 to 18, and the attitudes they reveal towards magical practices and techniques.

Most important magical teaching is to be found in the eighth verse:

Know you, how to rist, know you, how to read?
know you, how to colour, know you, how to test?
know you, how to ask, know you, how to bless?
know you, how to send, know you, how to sacrifice?

We've already remarked that eight is one of the principal magical numbers of runic magic, as the runes themselves are divided into aetts. We examine first, eight separate techniques which must be mastered by the rune-magician.

The first three, cutting, reading and staining. In order to cut runes you have to be able to read them, otherwise what you cut is gibberish.

The third technique, staining, was practised on many items, including standing stones, with traces of pigment enabling the original colouring to be reconstructed to red. Red is the colour of magic in many cultures, including our own. The Old Norse word *taufr* (talisman) and modern German *Zauber* (magic) come from a root meaning 'to make red' (a development which may actually have come from the practice of staining runes). Thus the reddening of the staves, either with actual blood or the red paint symbolizing it, is the specific action which loads them with power and gives them life, together with the chanting of the rune-name, which is the stave's breath as the red stain is its blood.

'Cutting' for magical purposes involved a concentration on the characters being cut to liberate their powers in the mind of the runemaster. It would have been a ritual in itself, with the runes being chanted to accompany the action: as the runes are scored in the earthly wood or stone, they are also cut in the World-Tree's roots, within the Well of Wyrd.

'Reading' involved knowing the runes and their correspondences, to ensure that what was being cut, be it for secular or magical purposes, was appropriate. The runic names, of course, were the most important of these. There is also a close correspondence to the modern sense of 'reading', i.e. consulting for divination.

'Testing' referred to both the runes being cut and the person doing the cutting. The concept of magical initiation is as valid for a runemaster as for anyone else, and the knowledge imparted orally and in practical demonstration would only have been communicated to the worthy, who would have to 'prove' their worth. One must of course be thoroughly versed in runecraft in order to be able to test someone before accepting them as apprentice.

'Asking' can refer to the wisdom to ask the right questions of the runes — questions that can be answered within the scope of rune-casting — and can also mean to 'invoke'. The Old Norse word used here, *bidja*, can also, in some contexts, mean to direct (cognate to English 'bid'). In both cases, the skill required is that of understanding the runes, and the gods themselves and the function they are meant to fulfil; it is no use asking, or bidding, them against their nature.

'Blessing' has to do with the consecration of the symbols used, each of which, whilst a component, made up a magical whole. The word used here, *blóta*, can (and usually does) mean to sacrifice to the gods, or worship through sacrifice, but it also signifies hallowing or dedicating something to a specific end.

'Sending' refers to the actual activation of the completed runecharm, the making-it-do-its-job part of the process. Like any other form of spell, a runecharm needs to be directed, and whilst this could be assumed in the purposeful way in which the charm is created, the extra reinforcement of the completed charm ensures an inescapable certainty equivalent to a statement of intent.

'Sacrificing' refers to the process by which the strength of the runester is poured into the runes: the more you give, the stronger your results are. The runes can be made to be work by types of physical 'sacrificing', as well; for instance, by carving

and staining them lightly, then scraping them into a drink or other magical substance meant to be empowered by them.

The eighteen 'Hávamál' charms form the longest extant list in any recorded sequence. Because of its range the 'Hávamál' list is the best to work with at this stage. If we examine each in turn we will discover its use and, in many cases, some hints as to its application.

The first is an uplifter, bringing cheer back during periods of illness or depression.
Runes applied to activate this charm are: Fehu, Inguz and Wunjo.

The second is a charm for leechcraft, and complements the first. Its use will enable the user to become skilled in the healing arts.
Runes: Uruz, Sowulo, Laguz.

The third is a battle charm, preventing adversaries from harming the possessor in conflict. It would most likely have been worn as a talisman, possibly in such a way, and of such material, to make its presence obvious, thus providing a psychological advantage to the wearer.
Runes: Thurisaz, Isa, Nauthiz.

The fourth is a charm which, because it relates to freeing oneself from bonds, does not actually require cutting. The runes could be employed in other ways, as sound vibrations and mental tuning devices, in addition to being cut, stained, etc. Odin uses the verb 'galdra', specifically implying that this enchantment is meant to be sung.
Runes: Ansuz, Fehu, Eihwaz.

The fifth turns a flying missile from its harmful course and sends it harmlessly to earth, assuming it is spotted in time. This is a protective device, to neutralize malicious magic and psychic self-defence.
Runes: Kenaz, Isa, Raido, Jera, Dagaz.

The sixth is a counter-magic spell. Using this charm will invoke the much-vaunted Law of Return, by which a thwarted spell rebounds upon its caster.

Runes: Hagalaz, Jera, Raido, Nauthiz, Thurisaz.

The seventh is a fire-extinguisher, and we may interpret this as a spell to intervene in a situation where a cool head is needed, for example to avoid a violent confrontation.

Runes: Isa, Laguz, Nauthiz, Gebo, Wunjo.

The eighth: strife between folk was one of the main hazards of Germanic life. The custom of feud, only somewhat mitigated by the processes of Thing (the judgement assembly) and the paying of weregild, brought many great heroes to grief. The Germanic people were (and still are) a bunch of proud, touchy individualists. This charm was, and is, indeed a very needful one to know.

Runes: Gebo, Mannaz, Wunjo.

The ninth: for a seafaring people such as the Vikings, this spell, which kept ships afloat and brought them to safe harbour, was another important one. It provides an instance of weather magic in a specific environment, and as the North Sea was the main adversary of any voyage from the Northern lands, it was an essential for seafarers who wanted to see home again.

Runes: Gebo, Raido, Ehwaz, Laguz.

The tenth: the translation here is ambiguous, with some scholars citing ghosts and others citing witches. Both of them were known to ride on top of house-roofs at night. Northern myth and magic played a formative part in the creation of the Medieval witch-myth, and broomstick-riders spring readily to mind. There is also an implication of shape-shifting into bird form, as both the hides and the souls of the garth-riders have to be sent home.

Runes: Ehwaz, Dagaz, Laguz.

The eleventh: another spell for protection in battle. The fact that the spell is chanted does not necessarily mean it wasn't written first. It is chanted behind the shield, and could well form part of the back of the shield. Tacitus mentions that Germanic warriors preparing for battle had a special cry, called the 'baritus', from which they could read how the battle would turn, and comments that, 'the object they specially seek is a certain volume of hoarseness, a crashing roar, their shields being brought up to their lips, that the voice may swell to a fuller and deeper note by means of the echo.'

Runes: Ansuz, Sowulo, Algiz.

The twelfth is real necromancy. Hanging was the primary method of sacrifice to Odin, as well as a means of execution. Here we have runes both written and stained to bring the victim back to life. Communicating with the dead.

Runes: Hagalaz, Kenaz, Eihwaz, Ansuz.

The thirteenth: the act of pouring water would have been the 'sending' part of this charm. This process, magically recreating the name-giving day in which the nine-day-old infant received name, doom and gifts, allows the setting of an Órlog ('fate') against harm in battle upon a young warrior. This can be repeated in a ritual where one accepts a new magical name, for example as part of an initiation ceremony.

Runes: Perthro, Laguz, Berkana, Othala.

The fourteenth tells us of the close ties between Germanic religion and Germanic magic. To be able to work in the worlds of the astral means to know the mighty ones who dwell there, when to call on them, how to befriend them, and how to read the messages they send us. Both the Gods and the elves, and other beings are important for the rune magician to deal with and understand.

Runes: Eihwaz, Mannaz, Ansuz.

The fifteenth is an unusual charm in that our narrator (Odin) acknowledges it came from another. Thjodrerir is a dwarf who doesn't appear elsewhere in the Elder Edda. A literal translation of Delling is 'shining'; his door is the dawn light. Dwarves traditionally turned to stone at dawn; but in addition to Thjodrerir, the charm is also of benefit to the Gods and elves and Odin, and presumably human beings as well.

Runes: Raido, Kenaz, Sowulo.

The sixteenth charm is written from a male point of view, but can work for either sex. This is making the desired one do the right thing by your inclinations, and shows the role sexual magic had to play in Northern society. This is the charm for getting your lover.

Runes: for a male — Kenaz, Inguz, Nauthiz; for a female — Thurisaz, Kenaz, Nauthiz.

The seventeenth is the charm for keeping your lover once you've used 16 to get her (or him). Again, singing doesn't negate the possibility that the eight stages described above are implicit in creating the charm. It simply means that its oral recitation activated the charm.

Runes: Gebo, Ehwaz, Wunjo.

The eighteenth is the hardest of all to interpret or comment upon. The only members of the opposite sex to whom it may be told are blood siblings or committed mates. This implies it has a personal power which remains personal and powerful whilst its secrecy is maintained. Its purpose is probably to promote a personal union, either with the beloved or with other aspects of oneself.

This is a personal combination of runes which is a secret for each individual to discover.

Any act of active magic is best done in a sacred and secure space, assuring protection from all negative possible influences both from within as well as from outside.

For this purpose, a simple format has been developed and has now been in use for a number of years, proving its effectiveness.

THE RUNIC CIRCLE

All your rituals should begin with the casting of a runic circle, both to ward yourself and to draw up and concentrate the might of the runes for your use. Regular casting of the circle has several effects. Firstly, when you start magical studies, you start giving off more energy and, at the same time, become more sensitive — you shine through the Inner Planes as an unwarded beacon, which can draw all sorts of nastiness and unwanted attention. The regular casting of a runic circle protects you from such things. Also, as you practise it, you will become more and more used to the sounds, shapes and magical feelings of each of the runes.

Begin by standing with feet together and hands at your sides, facing north. Raise your wand, ritual knife, or your strong hand and trace the stave-shape of Fehu, chanting 'Fehu, Fehu, Fehu' as you see a bright beam of red might springing from you and shaping the stave to burn in the air before you. Make this a big, bold gesture, with the bottom of the stave at groin-level and the top at head-level — you are putting your whole strength into it, so don't hold back or be cowardly about it. If circumstances do not permit you to chant at the top of your lungs, intensity must do in place of volume.

Turn to the northeast with your arm still held straight out, seeing a line of red might forming an arc from north to northeast, trace Uruz and chant it thrice. Continue through the first aett thus, until you are surrounded by a burning circle marked at the eight directions with runes: Thurisaz eastward, Ansuz south-east, Raido south, Kenaz south-west, Gebo west, Wunjo north-west.

Finish the circle at the north. Not losing sight of the Fehu rune burning in front of you, send your energy through its heart to trace a Hagalaz rune behind it as you chant 'Hagalaz' thrice. Do the second aett in the same manner, as a second circle outside the first. When you reach the north again, still aware of the Fehu and Hagalaz burning before you, send your energy out one more step to shape Teiwaz as you chant its name thrice, and continue with the third aett.

When you have closed off the third circle, stand for a moment, seeing the threefold ring of runes about you. Then trace the sign of the Hammer, seeing a huge Hammer-sign of blazing lightning spring forth outside the Fehu-Hagalaz-Teiwaz triad as you chant, 'Hammer ward me, wherever I go!' Repeat the Hammer-signing and the chant in each of the eight directions.

When you have reached the North again, reach over your head and trace a deosil (sunwise or clockwise) swastika in glowing white light (or, if you have not yet come to emotional terms with the misuse of this mighty sign by the Nazis, another Hammer-sign), chanting, 'Hammer shall always hallow my ways!' See the sign spinning faster and faster, funnelling a flood of brilliant whiteness down into your red circle. The crown of your head should tingle with this energy.

Below you, trace a widdershins (counter sunwise or counter clockwise) swastika (or Hammer) in glowing black light, chanting, 'Hammer shall always hallow my ways!' See the sign spinning faster and faster, funnelling a flood of brilliant blackness up into your red circle. The soles of your feet should tingle with this might.

Lift head and hands so that you stand in the shape of an Algiz-rune and cry, 'Above me Asgard's awesome might!'

Spread your feet shoulder-width apart and cry, 'Roots below in Hella's realm!'

Bring your feet together and lower your arms until you stand with them stretched out in the shape of a cross. Chant, 'Rune-might ringed around me, rune-might roar within me. Rune-might wards me, works my will wherever I shall go!' Stand still for a moment, eyes closed if needful, seeing the whole ring as a burning triple wheel whose spokes are the eight runic triads and Hammers, whose axle is you yourself between the whirling swastikas. The rune ring is now set and will move everywhere with you.

There is a simpler form of this ritual: chant and trace with your magical tool or your index finger, the runes in a complete circle around you, starting with Fehu in the North and ending with Dagaz. Then make the Hammer sign on the four quarters and invoke the protection of Thor. For example. 'Hammer in the North hallow and protect this space, hammer in the East, etc, etc.' When working in the Northern tradition always start North; if you use a harrow or altar place this in the North.

The regular practice of either of these rituals will put you in close touch with the runes and give great protection in every given situation.

Once the circle has been set up one can, in total safety, work magic, healing and/or divination.

Protective signs are the runes Algiz, Thurisaz and Dagaz.

Algiz on the four quarters keeps unwanted influences out.

Thurisaz acts likewise but can be activated as a self-guided missile, slinging all unwanted influences back to source.

Dagaz can hide the circle between the worlds. A specific strong combination is Algiz and Dagaz combined: ᛉ or ᛉ

Two more protective signs are known and used in Germanic magic:

a) A Thor's hammer:

b) The 'Helm of Awe':

The first can be bought as jewellery and worn on the body for continuous protection, the second is visualized on the forehead, especially effective in confrontational situations.

RUNES FOR ACTIVATING THE CHAKRAS

From virtually every mystery tradition, we learn about psychic energy centres or vortices in the physical/emotional/mental bodies, interconnecting these. These are mostly known by their sanskrit name, 'chakra', however in the Northern Tradition they have become known as 'Hvels', meaning wheels. For now we will use the more widely used 'chakra'.

There are many different theories as to how many of these centres there actually are. The traditional view promoted by Theosophy in the last century was that there were seven chakras. Some other esoteric traditions postulate that there are as many as twelve, some of which are not located on the Earth plane. We are going to work with eight: the seven well-known ones and in addition the one below the feet, the taproot chakra, which for the sake of not altering the conventional numbering of the seven chakras, I have designated the Zero chakra.

This exercise is experimental, so feel free to alter the runic order relating to the chakras in accordance with your insight.

Zero chakra: Located beneath one's feet extending as a taproot into the Inner earth. The Rune Hagalaz allows you to access this realm and draw energy from there.

First chakra: The base chakra associated with sense of identity and security. Isa is one of the runes which can be used to activate this chakra.

Second chakra: Traditionally associated with sexuality, pleasure and procreation, also in a creative sense. Nauthiz is most fitting to be used.

Third chakra: The chakra of power and will. Either Eihwaz or Jera will do, even better both as a bind-rune, Eihwaz as the spine and Jera circling around this, somewhere around the waist.

Fourth chakra: The heart chakra. To activate this, Sowulo is a mighty force.

Fifth chakra: Throat chakra, the chakra of communications: Gebo as well as Ansuz are two of the best runes to use to activate this chakra and improve communication on all levels.

Sixth chakra: The Third eye. Inguz chanted and projected into this space will develop clairvoyant abilities, if present.

Seventh chakra: The crown. Dagaz, as the rune of enlightenment, will facilitate understanding and processing of information obtained from higher levels of consciousness.

There are other runes which are very good in connection with various chakras but I suggest you find these for yourself by experimentation. As long as you are in a secured space you are unlikely to come to any harm. This is an exercise for which one may create a daily schedule and keep records of results obtained, changes of consciousness and/or dream space. Also these chakra exercises can improve one's health and personal stamina a great deal.

First, one must be able to *feel* these chakras: where they are situated and whether and in which direction they are spinning. Exercises for this can be found in many books for beginners; especially recommended is *Wheels of Life* by Anodea Judith, someone I have worked with, who is both knowledgeable and reliable.

Practise the chanting, singing and whispering of runes, see them taking shape while you are doing this. Develop visualization of runes; visualization exercises can also be found in most esoteric books for beginners. Once you master these two disciplines, chant and visualize the rune either from above your head or from under your feet, and draw this up to the chakra you're working with. Feel the rune settle here, leave it for a while, and then note what you feel, both physically and emotionally. Work steadily on this, as the results will be interesting and worthwhile.

GUIDED MEDITATION TO HELLA'S REALM

From the Caballah we have become familiar with the concept of 'pathworkings'. This means, literally, travelling on the interconnecting paths given in the traditional Cabalistic teachings on their version of the Tree of life.

Well, we've got a Tree of life of our own, and within the Norse mythology is given an exact description of the nine different realms and where they are located. Why would that be, if not to suggest that in at least some of the shamanic traditions of the North these paths were also explored?

Incidentally, I must state categorically that the further or deeper one gets into a mystery system, whatever it may be, the more one realizes the similarities suggesting that there is a universal principle behind them all and that they are localized versions of Mystery teachings of a Higher order. This for the benefit of people who have known me to work exclusively in my own ancestral and ethnic traditions. All ethnic traditions have similarities and possible similar origins in a different time span, at least from a linear perspective, and they can and will interface in the forthcoming Age of enlightenment.

PATHWORKING TO HELLA'S REALM

First of all this is never to be done alone. Always have a trusted companion with you and preferably a tape recorder running. The pathworking below is used to obtain communication with the shamanic underworld, ie the realm of the dead. The reason that one is warned not to undertake this alone is that the experience one undergoes can be extremely intense, and recollection may be very difficult after one returns. It is not actually dangerous in the physical sense unless one has an already existing health problem such as a weak heart, but psychologically it is dangerous to venture out in such uncharted territory without a guide.

Get as relaxed as possible, by whatever means you are used to. If you are not trained at all in this, join a meditation centre or a Yoga school. Once you are totally relaxed, visualize yourself in an environment in nature, a place if possible from memory where you really felt good. When ready give a pre-arranged sign to your companion to start the narration.

Below is the text to be read out by your companion, while you follow the instructions.

'You stand outside with your eyes closed. The breeze rustles softly through your hair; you smell the green scents of grass and leaves, feel the steady might of the earth beneath your feet.

'Now you open your eyes. You are standing in a place well known to you, a natural stead, far from cities and roadways, where you feel at home and at one with the earth.

'After you have stood gathering your strength for a few moments, you begin to walk. The way leads you on towards a woodland — grass rising to bushes at the path's edges, bushes to small trees, small trees to greater trees. The sunlight shines through the branches arching above the way, dappled by leaf-shadows that shift with every breeze. As you go further, the trees become older and thicker, the pathway darkening beneath the shade of their great limbs and heavy leaves.

'Ahead of you lies a clearing. In the middle of the clearing rises the greatest tree of all — an ancient yew, red berries shining like drops of blood against its dark needles. It is so tall that you cannot see its crown, only the grey clouds streaming about it like tails of foam; its roots rise higher than your head, and sink deeper into the earth than you can guess. You walk about the tree to the north. There, beneath one of the roots, you see a dark cave. You step within, breathing in the musty scent of the yew's bark as you make your way downward through the blackness.

'As you go, you begin to hear the clanging of metal — of hammer striking anvil, steel ringing from stone, iron clashing with gold. The sparks glimmer through the darkness all about you, flying from the anvils of the Swart-Alfs as they forge swords and helms, rings and spears and shield-bosses; the eyes of the dwarves glow red. You follow your path along, downward and to the east.

'The wind from the east is cold and raw with the storms of spring slapping icily against your face. Far off, you hear the thundering of the giants and rime-thurses casting boulders through the air, the sound of rocks cracking beneath their feet as they stride through the vast wastelands of Jotunheim; their shapes are shadows among the crags. But you are on the path that keeps you safe; you follow it along, downwards and to the south.

'The wind from the south is dry and burning-hot, crackling with sparks from the darkness as it sears your face. The leaping flames light the southern way — the all-devouring flames of the Muspilli, that will eat the world at the end of time; the sparks from Muspelheim hiss about you on the hot desert wind, and you can hear the fiery laughter of Surt's sons. But you are on the path that keeps you safe; you follow it along, downwards and to the south.

'The wind from the west is damp and cool, salty with the smell of the sea and rich with the scents of moist earth. From

PRINCIPLES OF RUNES

western Vanaheim, you hear the crashing of the waves against the shore and the soft evening lowing of cattle; glimmers of gold glint from the dark earth about you. But still you follow your path, down and to the north.

'Now the shadows on your way grow deeper. From the darkness, you hear the running of waters — large streams and small, some winding slowly and some rushing in torrents from the fells. You must step over the lesser streams, wade through the greater. Some are hot and stink of sulphur; some freeze your feet with the cold of mountain ice, but all must be crossed.

'Ahead of you, you hear the rushing of a much greater river, like a stormwind through trees. Beneath the sound of its frothing waters, you hear the clashing of weapons — sword on sword, spear on shield, steel clanging against rock, blade ringing against iron blade. The river runs sharp-edged with weapons, beating the lead-grey waters to froth in white rivulets about the harsh rocks. It is too deep and fierce to ford; you must follow the path on to where a huge boulder stands shadowy by the side of the steel bridge.

'A shape rises beside the boulder — a great woman's shape, roughly wrought in craggy grey stone. This is Modhgudhr, the giant-maid who wards the bridge to Hel. She speaks to you in a deep harsh voice like rock grating on rock, asking who you are and what you are doing here; you must answer her.

'When you have answered the giant-maid's challenge, you stride forth over the steel bridge. Cross boldly and it will be a wide and easy way; should your feet falter, it will be narrow and keen as the edge of a sword. Your tread rings from the steel as if a whole host rode with you — but a host of the dead would not make it ring so; it sounds only beneath the feet of the living.

'On the other side, a huge black wall rises before you, its shadow falling cold and dark across your face. You stand at the northern march of Hel; the wall wards the way. You start walk-ing towards the east, following the slow dark curve of the wall.

'At the east is a huge gate, black oak bound with bars of black iron. As you gaze at it, it swings slowly open: the land of Hel, of night and mist, lies before you.'

[Here your companion asks you questions: 'what do you see, is there a path, is there an animal, a human, are there trees, flowers?' Keep voice contact with your companion at all times, do not allow yourself to drift off. When you feel you've had enough, indicate this to your companion with your pre-arranged signal. To return, your companion reads:

'The gates of Hel swing closed behind you. You follow the path back around to the north, crossing the ringing bridge. Modgudr lets you pass freely; the path turns upwards and towards the west, over the many waters you crossed before. You leap the smaller and ford the greater, following the path about and up. The salty damp winds of Vanaheim blow against your face; upward and south, you pass again through the burn-ing wind of Muspelheim; upward and east, through the raw harsh winds of Jotunheim. Now you hear the hammering of the dwarves again, steel and stone, and see the glowing fires of their forges. Above you is the cave-mouth where you came in, a ring of light beneath the black roots of the tree; you climb upward, stepping out from under the arching root and blinking against the brightness of day. Slowly you follow the path back through the woods — old trees giving way to younger trees, younger trees to saplings, saplings to bushes, bushes to grass — until you reach the stead where you began. You stand there for a few moments, breathing in the soft breath of the wind, feeling your feet firmly rooted in the earth, your soul firmly rooted within your body, your self whole and one within the Middle-Garth's Ring.'

PRONUNCIATION OF RUNIC NAMES

The Rune names of the Elder Futhark are derived from the oldest Germanic language, before this separated itself into West Germanic and North Germanic languages. West Germanic languages include English, Dutch, Frisian. North Germanic languages are the Scandinavian languages. All through this book the word 'Germanic' is used purely as a linguistic term, without any connotations of 'race'.

The pronunciation of the Rune names of the Elder Futhark is relatively simple: there are only five vowel sounds and the consonants, with the exceptions below, are as in Modern English. Vowels:

a   as in 'father'
e   ay, as in 'day'
i   ee, as in 'reed'
o   as in 'home'
u   oo, as in 'moon'

Consonants:

dh	soft th, as in 'leather'
g	always hard, as in 'give'
h	may be heavily aspirated, almost as a 'ch'
j	always pronounced as y
k	always a hard sound; no soft c exists
r	trilled
th	as in 'thorn'
z	always buzzed, halfway between r and z

MISCELLANEOUS
INFORMATION

I f we examine the meaning of each rune's name we shall find it falls into one of eight categories:

1 *Animal:* Fehu — cattle; Uruz — aurochs (ure-ox — now extinct); Eihwaz — horse; Mannaz — man.
2 *Supernatural:* Thurisaz — giant; Ansuz — god (generally thought to be Odin); Teiwaz — the god Tyr; Inguz — the god Frey; Algiz — ritual enclosure, protection.
3 *Human activity:* Raido — riding, journeying.
4 *Objects:* Kenaz — torch; Gebo — gift; Perthro — fruit; Othala — inheritance.
5 *Human conditions:* Wunjo — joy, perfection; Nauthiz — need.
6 *Natural phenomena:* Hagalaz — hail; Isa — ice; Sowulo — sun; Laguz — water.
7 *Trees:* Eihwaz — yew; Berkana — birch.
8 *Times:* Jera — year, harvest; Dagaz — day.

RUNIC AROMATIC CORRESPONDENCES

Rune	Correspondence	Rune	Correspondence
Fehu	Spearmint, Cinnamon	Eihwaz	Cypress, Benzoin
Uruz	Cypress, Oakmoss	Pertho	Yarrow, Nutmeg
Thurisaz	Angelica, Frankincense	Algiz	Juniper, Peppermint
Ansuz	Cedar, Clove	Sowulo	Bay, Sandalwood
Raido	Basil, Vetivert	Teiwaz	Thyme, Lemongrass
Kenaz	Pine, Ginger	Berkana	Geranium, Dill
Gebo	Patchouli, Cardamom	Ehwaz	Grapefruit, Pettigrain
Wunjo	Marigold, Chamomile	Mannaz	Ylang-Ylang, Orange
Hagalaz	Rose, Lemon	Laguz	Jasmine, Myrrh
Nauthiz	Eucalyptus, Black Pepper	Inguz	Fennel, Melissa
Isa	Lavender, Yarrow	Othala	Marjoram, Neroli
Jera	Rosemary, Bergamot	Dagaz	Clary Sage, Linden Blossom

An example of using these correspondences:
A healing bind-rune — Uruz, Jera and Sowulo
Cypress 3 drops
Rosemary 1 drop
Sandalwood 1 drop
Base oil of choice, this is ideal for a 10ml blend.

SAFETY DATA

Essential oils should not be ingested and should be diluted in a base oil prior use.

A recommended oil-to-base ratio is 10 drops to 10ml of base oil. Neat oils may be added to an oil burner or incense blend.

Care must be taken with citrus oils such as Lemon or Bergamot as they can be harmful to the skin.

During pregnancy or breastfeeding oils should be well diluted and certain oils should be avoided altogether, such as: Basil, Cinnamon, Marjoram, Fennel, Juniper, Thyme, Peppermint, Rosemary, Clove, Nutmeg, Bay, Black Pepper, Cedar.

NB: A good book on aromatherapy can give great insight into the use of essential oils and more information on their safe use.

THE TWELVE PALACES OF ASGARD AND THEIR CORRESPONDENCE TO THE ASTROLOGICAL SIGNS AND HOUSES

L ike the magical number nine, twelve also seems to have a special significance in Northern mythology. In Asgard, we find twelve palaces, and the gods who dwell in each one. These twelve palaces can be superimposed on the twelve astrological houses. The twelve palaces are listed below with associated signs of the zodiac.

Palace	Astrological Sign
Bilskinir	Aries
Thrymheim	Taurus
Folkvang	Gemini
Himminbjorg	Cancer
Breiablikk	Leo
Sokkvabekk	Virgo
Glitnir	Libra
Gladsheim	Scorpio
Ydalir	Sagittarius
Landvidi	Capricorn
Valaskjalf	Aquarius
Noatun	Pisces

EXPLORING FURTHER

THE RING OF TROTH EUROPE

A FELLOWSHIP OF THE KINDRED OF THE AESIR AND VANIR

The Ring of Troth is a network of folk who follow the Heathen traditions of the Germanic peoples. Currently based in the UK, the Ring of Troth Europe has members in many European countries.

Membership of the Ring of Troth is open to anyone who sincerely wishes to participate, regardless of race, gender, ethnic origin, sexual orientation or other divisive criteria. The Ring of Troth aims to promote personal and collective awareness of our interdependence with the living world. We work together with other groups fighting to preserve the Earth and protect it from the forces of destruction.

Members receive a regular newsletter *From the Hearth*, including news of events and contact information.

For further information The Ring of Troth Europe can be contacted as follows:

Ring of Troth
BM Troth
London WC1N 3XX
e-mail: aclifton@btinternet.com
website: www.troth.org.uk

Freya Aswynn can be contacted for readings, either postal,
in person or on-line via her website. Also planned are runic
residential workshops and a new correspondence course is in
preparation.

All enquiries should be directed to:

Freya Aswynn
BM Aswynn
London WC1N 3XX
e-mail: aswynn@btinternet.com
Web: www.aswynn.co.uk

READING LIST

ESPECIALLY RECOMMENDED:

Northern Mysteries and Magick by Freya Aswynn, published by Llewellyn, USA

Teutonic Magic by Kveldulfr Gundarsson, published by Llewellyn, USA

Teutonic Religion by Kveldulfr Gundarsson, published by Llewellyn, USA

Northern Magic Runic Mysteries and Shamanism by Edred Thorsson, published by Llewellyn, USA

Futhark by Edred Thorsson, published by Samuel Weiser, USA

Runelore by Edred Thorsson, published by Samuel Weiser, USA

At the Well of Wyrd by Edred Thorsson, published by Samuel Weiser USA

Helrunar by Jan Fries, published by Mandrake, Oxford, UK

Anglo-Saxon Mythology, Migration and Magic by Tony Linsell, published by Anglo-Saxon Books, UK

ALSO FAIRLY USEFUL:

Rune Magic by Donald Tyson, published by Llewellyn, USA

Elements of the Runes by Bernard King, published by Element Books, UK